# The Wond[barcode]

*Music that changed the world*

*Sammy Stein*

First Published in Great Britain in 2022

Copyright © 2022 Sammy Stein

The author has asserted their right under the Copyright, Designs and Patent Act 1988 to be identified as the author of this work.

Published by the Independent Publishing Network

All rights reserved. No part of this book may be reproduced in any form or by any electronic or mechanical means, including information storage and retrieval systems, without permission in writing from the publisher, except by reviewers, who may quote brief passages in a review.

ISBN 978-1-80068-872-8 (print)

Website: sammystein.org

# CONTENTS

# INTRODUCTION

FROM HUMBLE BEGINNINGS in the streets and squares of New Orleans, jazz is now heard across the globe, whether in tiny venues, large halls, or at festivals with thousands watching. Jazz can be raw and untamed or sophisticated. The jazz scene in each country soaks up some of the local flavor, so it becomes unique to that place. Jazz has withstood wars, social upheaval, and periods when enthusiasm for live music waned. Despite the changing nature of how music is accessed and created, it remains ever-present. It is music that reflects society, echoes people's needs and desires, and gives release to emotions like no other genre.

This book is an immersive exploration of jazz's history, impact, and future. No matter how many papers, books, reviews, and interviews one reads, unanswered questions remain. Is jazz still relevant? How do musicians make enough money? What about gender issues? Just how many subgenres can there be?

Many books about jazz are written by observers, so to get an authentic account, I brought in those who play, produce, host radio shows, and record jazz music. Like jazz itself, this book had improvisational and collaborative aspects in its development.

Music is the loudest form of protest, and through it, people rise above societal expectations. It is also one of the great levelers, where background and monetary status count for nothing if you do not have the richness of talent. Jazz is embedded deep in the fabric of our lives and is arguably the most exciting music of our time. By reading this book, I hope you feel inspired to keep discovering what jazz offers.

If you believe jazz is historical music with predictable characteristics, you may be surprised. Jazz is energetic, profound, passionate, reactionary, and beautiful. The jazz of today is mind-blowing. Jazz people are not elite; they are you and me—all of us.

Some information in this book comes from months of research, but most comes directly from those in the music. After all, if you want to know about jazz, who better to ask than those who make their living from playing and teaching the music? Who else witnesses the reactions of an audience, understands how jazz music sells, or how relevant jazz is right now?

Jazz has influenced art, fashion, other music genres, and has absorbed elements from many cultures. It remains determined to make the world a better place, one note at a time.

What exactly is jazz, and how do you know you are listening to it? Do we truly know when and how jazz first originated? Who was the first jazz musician? How does jazz link to other genres? How has it affected society, and how does the future look? This book shows that today's jazz musicians and audiences are as colorful and diverse as the country that gave birth to it. Jazz is rising like a phoenix—beautiful, aflame, empowered by the knowledge of the ancients, and invigorated by the energy of youth. The young musicians coming into jazz question established canons and change the music from the inside out.

Many experts have written about the lives of great jazz musicians such as John Coltrane, Duke Ellington, Billie Holiday, Aretha Franklin, Horace Silver, and many others. You may discover that one musician had a physical deformity, which meant he took a particular stance when he played; another had a dental problem, which meant he had to give up the flute and switch to saxophone. Another went on stage so high on drugs that she collapsed; another had two children by the time she was fifteen. Two musicians hated each other but appeared as united brothers in public, and one kept her money in a bright red hatbox that she took everywhere— even on stage. Learning facts like these help us understand musicians' characters, but this book concentrates on the deeper parts of jazz.

Some people may think they know the answers to all things jazz. The truth is, they don't, and nor do I. Neither am I saying the book is fully comprehensive—no book on a topic as broad as jazz can be. I am writing for readers who want to understand more about jazz and be part of the energy—curious people with inquiring minds.

One of the beautiful public squares in New Orleans.

Photo credit: Sammy Stein

# CHAPTER 1

## Once upon a time in New Orleans

TOWARD THE END of the nineteenth century, New Orleans, Louisiana, was a busy trading center for goods coming from South America, Africa, Asia, and other places. It was a magnet for foreign business and traders. Newcomers and their families lived in the city and the surrounding districts. They joined people of Asian and European descent who had already made this part of America their home. There were also enslaved people, forcibly brought from other places and sold to dealers in human cargo. Many New Orleans residents owned slaves, for whom conditions were harsh.

A few years ago, I was shown around New Orleans by Carmela Rappazzo, a jazz singer from New York who now lives in the city. I asked about the small buildings attached to many of the grand houses in the Garden District, and Carmela explained that those would have been slave quarters.

Slavery in the southern states was nothing new, of course, but in New Orleans, several things came together to create a unique environment. Perhaps, looking back, we can see how conditions had been perfect for something new to be born.

## A BIT OF JAZZ HISTORY

THE ACCEPTED STORY of jazz goes something like this: In New Orleans, a city of mixed cultures, people socialized, played music, and danced. The music evolved with the mixing of rhythms from cultures of the free and enslaved. The instruments were often homemade or purchased from pawnshops after Confederate soldiers returned from war. The first jazz musician was New Orleans resident Charles 'Buddy' Bolden, a barber and cornet player. The music became jass, then jazz, and spread north across America, helped by the bands that played on the riverboats plying the network of rivers radiating from the Mississippi. Jazz developed from this "melting pot" of cultures. Jazz rhythms originated in African dance patterns and emerged at the beginning of the twentieth century. Exactly where the name jass, which was jazz's original name, came from is unclear, but it may have been from the jasmine perfume women wore in brothels, where many jazz musicians began their careers. Jass was also a lewd term for a female bottom.

However, the whole truth about how jazz came to be is far more complex...

## FRENCH AND SPANISH INFLUENCES

BECAUSE OF ITS French and Spanish heritage, Louisiana imported slaves from the colonies of Benin, Congo, and Senegal, so the cultural mix was diverse. France controlled Louisiana from 1682 until 1762, when it was ceded to Spain. "*Code noir*" was applied during French rule, and the "Law of Coartación" was practiced under Spanish rule. Coartación allowed enslaved people to earn money and purchase their freedom. Both of these systems influenced the demographics and society of the region.

---

### Code Noir

*Code noir* imposed strict rules regarding slavery within the French colonies and transferred them to New Orleans when it was under French control. For example, slaves were obliged to receive Roman Catholic instruction, Sundays were rest days, and the state could confiscate slaves found working on a Sunday. Mixed marriages and cohabitation were banned. Some masters abused female slaves, and any children produced as a result were dubbed *mulatto*—a derogatory term for a person of mixed race. If a child was born to a slave as a result of sex between a slave and a master, both child and slave would be looked after by the state and never freed. However, if a child was born to a formerly enslaved person and a woman still enslaved, they should marry, and the enslaved woman would be freed. Slaves could marry with their master's permission, and the husband and wife were not to be separated. Any resulting children could stay with their parents until they were fourteen.

Under *Code noir*, slaves from different households were forbidden to gather. They could own no property, and theft could result in branding or other punishment. If a free person sheltered a runaway slave, they were fined and could be made slaves themselves. Life for enslaved people was harsh. Although they

---

were entitled to proper clothes, decent food, and fair treatment, and could report cruel treatment to the attorney general, what was considered cruel is unclear. When they became too old, ill, or were disabled and could no longer work, they were entitled to care in their masters' homes or at the local hospital, for which their masters paid a fee.

*Code noir* forbade the use of the rack, and putting slaves in irons was a last resort. Murder or injury of slaves was illegal, and masters over the age of twenty-five had the power to free their slaves. In theory, these freed slaves enjoyed the rights of any citizen. Those of mixed race were granted a status between black and white.

When Louisiana came under Spanish rule, the Law of Coartación allowed a slave to buy or earn their freedom. Gatherings could take place in public places. However, people of mixed race were reassigned black status, and the Spanish authorities refused to recognize freed slaves, despite them theoretically having the same status as any free person.

People of all statuses gathered in squares such as Congo Square (now Louis Armstrong Park). There are accounts of African ritualistic dances, known as "ring shouts," which were colossal, circular, wheeling dances that the slaves of African origin took part in, both in Louisiana and other states. In New Orleans, the city council gave over a designated area for slaves to gather and dance, which meant they remained in touch with their culture and heritage (in the surrounding states, the culture of slaves was largely ignored). With the convergence of so many cultures, classes, and artistic ideas, it was inevitable that something magical music-wise would happen.

New Orleans and its immediate vicinity had a singularity compared to the rest of America in another way related to jazz. During Coartación, if a slave played an instrument, they could earn a little money, so for slaves, learning an instrument may have been a means to buy their freedom.

The increase in the number of freed slaves and the multicultural demographic of New Orleans promoted exchanges of ideas and customs. Free and enslaved people lived in close proximity and would have heard many kinds of music played in the street and squares, and at important events. Despite integration not being officially allowed, the music of different cultures mixed. New Orleans proved then, as it does now, that it was a city with a unique character.

In 1803, Louisiana became part of the United States, and New Orleans saw an influx of freed slaves from other states. Those whose families had lived in America for two generations were called African-Americans, and the cultural mix became even more diverse.

## EARLY NINETEENTH CENTURY AND THE CIVIL WAR

SINCE ABOUT THE tenth century, improvisation has been used in music. For example, singers improvised against the tenor chant in Gregorian chants, and organists in churches added devised ornamentations to the score and passages between verses of hymns. Opera singers embellished passages with coloratura—heavily ornamented vocal passages. Since the fourteenth century, many composers have used syncopation in several genres, including European folk music. So syncopation (see Chapter 2) and improvisation had long been part of the musical heritage of people living around New Orleans.

As early as the 1850s, New Orleans composer Louis Moreau Gottschalk (1829–1869) wrote piano pieces that included Creole elements and characteristics we would attribute to early jazz. Gottschalk traveled extensively and incorporated Cuban, Columbian, and South American music elements into his compositions.

However, once music was written down, there was little allowance for improvisation. Musicians played what was in front of them and followed instructions, so improvisation became rarer. Gatherings in the streets and squares proved creative cauldrons because improvisation naturally occurs when musicians play or sing in a social setting without notated music or instructions. This means that elements of jazz music were already present and influenced players long before the end of the nineteenth century.

New Orleans had a history that differed from the surrounding states. Slavery was abolished in 1865 (apart from for some criminal offenses) when the 13th Amendment was ratified, which eventually led to greater freedoms in surrounding states, but in Louisiana, and especially in New Orleans, with its narrow streets where free and enslaved lived side by side, and with its diversity, there had already been decades of cultural mixing, so music evolved differently.

Does it not seem likely, given the mix of cultures, instruments, and rhythms the area thrummed with, that the music of New Orleans would develop its own character? Would not the multicultural environment have influenced the music played in the streets? Is it possible that music we might recognize as jazz was around long before it was labeled as such? Jazz grew from a cultural smorgasbord that only New Orleans, its colonial roots, and particular mix of people, combined with scant regard for strict enforcement of segregation policies, could provide.

During the Civil War (1861–1865), marching bands played instruments that needed to be portable, loud, and relatively easy to play. After the war, many of these instruments were abandoned or ended up in pawnshops in New Orleans. Ordinary people, including freed African-Americans, got hold of them, resulting in an almighty sound explosion. In a marching band, players could only play one drum at a time, so playing methods evolved, including the "second line," which involves two drummers—one for the up beat and one for the down. Together, the combinations of two beats created four- and eight-beat rhythm patterns frequently found in jazz music. Later, the same rhythms came to be used in boogie-woogie and rock and roll.

The invention of the bass pedal by New Orleans drummer Edward "Dee Dee" Chandler in 1896 changed everything; now, a continuous bass beat could be played, to which other rhythms could be added, and seated drummers could have a range of other drums around them. The drum set was born, allowing musicians to be even more inventive.

## The origins of jazz

WHEN I ASKED musicians how they thought jazz had come about, many pointed out that the complex elements that became incorporated into jazz could not have arisen spontaneously—they had to have been there already. Perhaps separate and in different music—classical, folk, and religious music, for example—but each element had to have been present in the history and culture of the people of New Orleans and came together to create the sounds we would know as jazz.

Musicians cited people they believed were influential in the development of syncopation and improvisation who are important because they introduced elements that would later become part of jazz. One named the seventeenth-century lutist John Dowland as creating the concept of improvisation. Others mentioned French composers Erik Satie and Claude Debussy and German composer Johann Sebastian Bach as jazz's forerunners. Satie, in particular, brought harmonic structure to the forefront in *Les Fils des Etoiles*, and the rhythm patterns in his *Gymnopedia No. 1* give his music anticipation and a hung (slightly held back) beat, which is often found in jazz. There were elements of jazz and ragtime in his music from as early as 1877 when he wrote *Trois Sarbanes* with dissonant harmonies and varied rhythms. Apparently, his scores contained instructions like "work it out for yourself," "light as an egg" and "open your head"—very jazz.

As early as the 1870s, rhythmic, syncopated music was played on violin, banjo, and upright bass at waterfront dance houses along the Ohio, Missouri, and Mississippi rivers. By the 1890s, small bands were playing all over New Orleans. It was only a matter of time before people would try to define and name the music.

By the late 1890s, there were attempts to write down jazz compositions. Once something is written down, parameters are drawn. The music is controlled by the people writing it, who may come up with original ideas and call themselves the composers or, as happened in early jazz, they may say they had composed the music when they had not. Now the music had something classical music had—documentation. Classical composers wrote down their music or used scribes and had done so for centuries, but many early jazz musicians were illiterate, so there were no "compositions" from these New Orleans music makers. This makes pinpointing jazz's emergence difficult, and oral accounts were relied on for many of jazz's early years. Once music is written down, it needs a label to identify it in catalogs.

Cornetist and bandleader Buddy Bolden from New Orleans is often said to have been the first jazz musician, yet we know this only from oral accounts. No recordings of his playing exist, and he was active only from 1900–1907 before being committed to an asylum due to mental illness. He was influenced by gospel music and blues. His outlandish behavior and loud, improvised blowing meant his legend lived long after he stopped playing.

Other musicians claimed to have invented jazz. Pianist, bandleader, and composer Ferdinand "Jelly Roll" Morton claimed he was the first to write down jazz music. His "Original Jelly Roll Blues" was published in 1915, and he is said to have claimed to have written jazz music down as early as 1902. Trumpeter, cornetist, and bandleader Nick LaRocca also claimed he was the first jazz composer, but the truth is, who knows?

## RAGTIME

THE NAME JAZZ was generally used by 1913, though the music had been around for some time before. From 1890 to 1917, ragtime was popular. Ragtime was music for banjo, and later piano, and it was often played in theaters and concert venues. Composers could make a small living selling their notated music. Scott Joplin's "Maple Leaf Rag" and James P. Johnson's "Harlem Strut" are examples. Minstrel shows featured ragtime music, singers, and actors, either black or in blackface (black makeup worn by white musicians to imitate black people), who would perform songs and short musical plays, often lampooning the powers that be.

The piano music had sophisticated rhythmic patterns, usually played by the right hand, with the left hand carrying a steady rhythm. Alongside ragtime, there was also blues music: jazz and blues share characteristics such as grace or "blue" notes and flattened intervals. Blues evolved more from field hollers, spiritual music, and a blend of major and minor harmonies. Some blues numbers, such as W.C. Handy's 1914 "St Louis Blues" (Columbia) and "Memphis Blues" (Victor Talking Machine), include so many jazz references they fit into lists of both genres.

## DIXIELAND AND JAZZ

THE MERGING OF blues and ragtime in the early 1900s, using simple harmonics, resulted in Dixieland jazz. Trumpeters Louis Armstrong and Henry "Red" Allen, trombonist Jack Teagarden, clarinetist Sidney Bechet, and pianists Earl Hines and Jelly Roll Morton were exponents of Dixieland. Eubie Blake, another Dixieland specialist, was discovered in 1907 playing at a brothel when he was fifteen by boxer Joe Gans, who asked him to play at the Goldfield Hotel.

At the same time that Bolden's band played in New Orleans dance halls, there were Freddie Keppard's Olympia Orchestra, the Superior, the Eagle Band (actually Bolden's band after he was hospitalized, led by trombonist Frankie Dusen, named after a saloon in New Orleans), and the Peerless. These bands featured players of note, such as cornetist King Oliver, trumpet player Bunk Johnson, and clarinetist Sidney Bechet.

"Papa Jack" Laine led mixed-race marching bands from the early 1900s. His Reliance Brass Band recruited many musicians who later became famous, including Nick LaRocca, tubist Chink Martin, and clarinetist Alcide Nunez. Laine had a long career that transcended Bolden's, and he was active long after Bolden faded. In 1916, a few members of his brass section got a gig at the prestigious Reisenweber's Cafe in New York. The café was famous for promoting cabaret and jazz. Columbia Gramophone Company recorded them but never released the record. However, the group—now called the Original Dixieland Jazz Band—made a recording for Victor Talking Machine Company in 1917. Titled "Livery Stable Blues," many cite it as the first jazz record.

Most dismissed LaRocca's claims to have written the piece, and a lawsuit to determine the composer found the origin of the music was so complex and challenging that no single writer could claim to have written the song. It was recorded by all-white members of Laine's band. This music of black musicians, heavily "borrowed" for the recording, sold millions of copies.

However, before "Livery Stable Blues," in Sydney, Australia, Billy Romaine advertised himself as a jazz musician. He was active beginning in 1914, and in 1918 a vaudeville act called Australia's First Jazz Band toured the eastern states around the same time. So the term "jazz" was in usage before 1917, putting LaRocca's claim of inventing it in the shade. Two weeks before the Original Dixieland Jazz Band went into Victor's studio, Arthur Collins and Byron Harlan recorded "That Funny Jas Band From Dixieland" on the same label. Borbee's Jass Orchestra released "It's a Long, Long Time" and "Just The Kind Of Girl You'd Love

To Make Your Wife" in February 1917 (Columbia)—both jazz records—followed by "The Ragtime Volunteers Are Off To War" in August 1917. There are other recordings from as early as 1914 made by W.C. Handy and the Prince's Band, led by bandleader and composer Charles Prince, which contain elements of jazz.

The quality of these early recordings was variable, in part, because the musicians had to gather in one space and play simultaneously into a large horn-shaped apparatus. With different instruments having different volumes, the only way to get an accurate recording was to position the musicians at different distances from the horn. A stylus then scratched the recording onto a shellac disc. Recording trills and rapid passages proved difficult, so these were often added later in the studio to enhance the sound.

Still, the recording of "Livery Stable Blues" by the Original Dixieland Jazz Band is the first widely acknowledged jazz record, and, for some, this was when jazz was born. But the band took ideas they heard and created pieces based on these, so the music had to exist long before. The Original Dixieland Jazz Band used publicity-grabbing stunts to draw large crowds to their performances, so it is no surprise their recording is remembered most. The record was symbolic of what became the norm for jazz: people with commercial savvy took the music and made money.

## JAZZ BEYOND LOUISIANA

WHATEVER THE TRUTH about its origin, jazz became Louisiana's greatest export. It traveled far beyond the web of rivers emanating from New Orleans. As it reached each metropolitan center, it took on board the local people's cultural influences, so jazz became different in New York, Detroit, and Chicago.

Chicago became another center of jazz, fueled by the arrival in 1915 of Papa Laine's band from New Orleans. Shortly after this, King Oliver, and later Louis Armstrong, moved to the city, helping make it a magnet for jazz musicians. Stellar artists emerged from the burgeoning jazz scene, including clarinetists Jimmie Noone and Johnny Dodds, drummer Baby Dodds, and guitarist/banjo player Johnny St. Cyr.

Kid Ory took his trombone and band to California in 1921, and became one of the first black recording artists, recording "Sunshine Blues" (Nordskog records). That same year, James P. Johnson recorded the first jazz piano solo record, "Carolina Shout" (Okeh Records). Jazz was catching on.

Sidney Bechet—formerly of Freddie Keppard's Olympia Orchestra in New Orleans and Will Marion Cooke's Syncopated Orchestra in New York—took his soprano saxophone and clarinet to France in 1925, where he found an appreciative audience. Not that this was his first visit to Europe. He had played in London in 1922 but was arrested for assault and deported on his release from jail. He had recorded "Wild Cat Blues" and "Kansas City Man Blues" in New York in 1923 as part of Clarence Williams' Blue Five. The group comprised cornetist Thomas Morris, pianist Clarence Williams, and soprano saxophonist Bechet, with the rest of the band's members varying according to different accounts. Some say trombonist John Mayfield and banjo player Buddy Christian were part of the group. Others cite pianist Stanley Miller and cornetist (later trumpet player) Louis Armstrong. "Wild Cat Blues" was an early recording of a composition by Thomas "Fats" Waller, who wrote it with Williams. In France, Bechet received warm welcomes whenever he returned, which he did throughout his career. His fortunes in America were mixed, some of this due to his recording contract, which limited events he could play. He eventually returned to France for good in 1950, and he lived there until his death in 1959.

The New Orleans Rhythm Kings made Dixieland recordings in Chicago, and Morton's Red Hot Peppers, led by Jelly Roll Morton, wowed audiences and recorded numbers including "Doctor Jazz" and "Black Bottom Stomp" (Victor 1926).

Initially, record companies had largely ignored black musicians, but during the late 1920s it became clear that there were different markets among black and white jazz lovers. Labels specialized in marketing some types of jazz and particular musicians, including Bessie Smith, Ruth Less, Mamie Smith, Lonnie Johnson, and Ma Rainey, via labels known as "race labels," which included Okeh, Vocalion, and Emerson, to one part of the population and other forms on different label imprints to the rest of America.

During the 1920s, larger bands began playing arrangements of jazz numbers that led to symphonic jazz, performed by an orchestra under a musical director. These included composer and arranger Paul Whiteman. Duke Ellington is acknowledged by many as the first great jazz composer, but Charles Ives had composed jazz pieces for orchestra as early as 1902, probably influenced by listening to his father's marching band. Debussy's "Golliwog's Cakewalk" of 1908, written as part of a suite in which toys he remembered as a child came to life, uses rhythm patterns from New Orleans' cakewalks—dances performed on New Orleans' streets and in minstrel shows. Other classical-jazz compositions include Maurice Ravel's violin sonatas and piano concertos. Hindemith's 1922 *Piano Suite op.26* has strong jazz references, as does Alban Berg's opera *Lulu* (1929). Francis Poulenc, Kurt Weill, Ernst Krenek, and Michael Tippett have all used jazz references in their compositions.

New styles of jazz came as more artists moved away from New Orleans. Armstrong now led his small ensembles—his Hot Five and Hot Seven combos that played powerful jazz with sweet overtones, underpinned by relentless rhythms and melodic phrasing. Earl Hines adapted Armstrong's style to the piano, creating a wavering effect with his right hand to create a cornet-like sound.

Duke Ellington took his band to New York in the early 1920s, and players, including saxophonist Johnny Hodges and trombonist Juan Tizol, added mutes (devices inserted into the ends of instruments to change or reduce the sound) made from all manner of items, including sink plungers, to create "jungle" sounds and growls.

Composer and pianist James P. Johnson's pupil, Thomas "Fats" Waller, became a renowned jazz pianist, and Fletcher Henderson and his dance band made jazz records. Big band dance music became increasingly popular, with its pendulous swinging rhythms and big horn sounds.

More white musicians began to play jazz. Bix Beiderbecke, a cornet player from Iowa, played with just about anyone who would let him, and he gained respect for his prowess and incredible improvisational skills. Beiderbecke and other white, middle-class players joined jazz bands and blurred the color barriers—Beiderbecke became the epitome of Chicago-style jazz.

Many dance bands, including Red Nichols and his Five Pennies, The Wolverines, and Frank Teschemacher's Chicago Rhythm Kings, played in ballrooms and on the radio. When sound was introduced to movies in 1927, these bands provided the perfect soundtrack, meaning jazz was heard widely.

Members of big swing bands would often form smaller ensembles and hold experimental jam sessions. Benny Goodman's band had one group comprising Goodman on clarinet, Teddy Wilson on piano, Gene Krupa on drums, and Lionel Hampton on vibraphone. Unlike the more extensive jam sessions after gigs, which could become highly competitive, these were respectful affairs to try out musical ideas before playing them in public.

## JAZZ DEVELOPS

IN THE 1930s, swing—danceable music arranged for big bands—became popular and swing band leaders included Benny Goodman, Tommy Dorsey, Cab Calloway, and Artie Shaw.

In the mid-1940s, groups began experimenting with jazz and taking it in new directions. Bebop included complex rhythms over which soloists would play difficult, technically demanding improvised sections. Many bebop numbers had a melodic opening with the ensemble playing in harmony, an improvised middle section, and a return to the melody toward the end. Bebop was popular with musicians because it offered them both ensemble playing and a challenge and a chance to shine in solo work. It allowed musicians to push boundaries yet had enough familiarity to keep audiences engaged. People enjoyed watching performers such as saxophonists Sonny Stitt and Dexter Gordon, bassist Ray Brown, and pianists Hank Jones and Bud Powell. Many jazz players listed as "great" are bebop players.

During the 1950s, Latin and Afro-Cuban music arose from the combination of bebop, ragtime, swing, and the addition of solid percussion. Singers, including Gloria Estefan and Shakira, have used Latin rhythms extensively in their songs. Numbers like Ricky Martin's "Livin' La Vida Loca" (Columbia 1999) may never have graced the charts had it not been for this jazz evolution.

By the late 1950s, jazz had fragmented into cool, bop, West Coast, swing, and trad subgenres. Each had supporters, and sometimes they developed an open dislike of fans of other subgenres. In the UK, this led to violent clashes between trad and modern jazz supporters (i.e. the Beaulieu jazz riot) in 1960. Small white ensembles took over the newer jazz styles, and it became cerebral and elite. Smooth, cool jazz was turned into academic music to be analyzed and dissected rather than spontaneous, reactionary music played in the moment.

In the mid-to-late 1960s, jazz developed its "cool" side, which directly opposed bebop and featured delicate extended lines with overlapping solos. Pianist Lennie Tristano, cornetist Leon "Bix" Beiderbecke, saxophonists Stan Getz and Gerry Mulligan, and trumpeters Shorty Rogers and Miles Davis played cool jazz. This was also when jazz became academic, and an eliteness crept into the music—something the original performers would have found surprising.

From the mid-1960s onwards, free jazz, or free-form (or avant-garde), exploded onto the jazz scene. Free jazz featured experimental playing and improvisation, and players pushed at rules, harmony, and rhythm concepts. Yet, free-form jazz still features the return, follows key progressions, and contains a structure built around improvisation.

One musician I spoke with, bassist, composer, and researcher Rus Wimbish, stated, "Bolden gets the credit, mainly for adapting the blues to brass band instrumentation, inventing 'Big Four' beat, and leading an improvising band. Surely there were others, but oral histories credit Bolden as the best and most original."

Singer Deelee Dubé told me, "Jazz evolved from African-American folk songs, which then developed into ragtime, marches, blues, and other styles, which eventually culminated into the jazz art form. Subgenres include rock and roll, swing, third stream, Dixieland, bebop, and free jazz, fusion, funk, soul, Latin jazz, Afro-jazz, soul jazz, pop, jazz, and so on."

Another musician I spoke with, pocket trumpeter Pierre-Emmanuel Seguin, seemed to sum up the thoughts of many quite well: "It was probably a group of people rather than one, and their names might stay unknown forever."

Musician and reviewer Joe Higham added, "I'd suspect pinning jass/jazz down to one person, or even a group, would

> be almost impossible."
> Radio station owner Anthea Redmond added pertinently,
> "What a brave question. You could probably start a war with this!"

\*\*\*

JAZZ IS STILL young as a genre. There are people alive who played with the great pioneering jazz musicians. Only three years ago, I was in Quito, Ecuador, asking questions of Marvin "Doc" Holladay, now a Quito resident, who played with Duke Ellington. He had opinions on many subjects, including who were the best female jazz vocalists. There are musicians who played with John Coltrane, Ornette Coleman, and other jazz greats. I recently saw Wayne Shorter in concert with Wynton Marsalis. Shorter played with Miles Davis and many other jazz luminaries. Archie Shepp is another player who played with celebrated jazz greats of the past. He recently performed at the London Barbican Centre, as part of the London Jazz Festival. While researching an article for the Library of Congress on Sweet Emma Barrett, I recently spoke with Doctor Henry Blackburn, who accompanied

In New Orleans, any corner in even a tiny bar can be a stage.

Photo credit: Sammy Stein

Barrett and the Preservation Hall Band on tour in the mid-1960s. These are all reminders that great jazz musicians, who we consider pioneers, are only a generation back.

Jazz has changed much in the short time it has existed. We have not yet had time to see jazz fully develop, or to explore all the possibilities it holds, and new opportunities keep presenting themselves. Veterans and newcomers bring new ideas, and watching jazz evolve is one of the most interesting musical journeys it is possible to make. Jazz "history" is still being created, so documenting interviews—with the great musicians of today and those who played with jazz's past greats—is important.

However, we have to be careful about defining jazz, because once we define anything, we limit its potential to grow beyond our expectations. There is always more to explore, different challenges, new ways to play, a feel to find, so it is unlikely you will ever reach a point where you feel you fully understand jazz. And that is fine. I would advise getting to know the basics, then just listening, opening up, and allowing the music to take you where it will.

Most musicians I spoke with concluded that it is best left undecided as to who was the first jazz musician and the exact nature of jazz's origins. Accounts are sketchy and vague because no one was writing about jazz when musicians began playing it. Not only that, it was just one kind of music of many that would have been heard. For musicians, it is more about learning and maintaining an open mind. In any case, what difference would it make if we could pinpoint the precise moment jazz evolved or provide a name for the first musician to play jazz?

Jazz originated not in one particular spot or time. Once born, its spread was phenomenal, and now there is hardly a musician who has not been touched by jazz. Instead of a timeline leading to one spot where we can point and state, "this is where jazz was born," jazz's timeline leads to a starburst of possibilities—and perhaps that is what makes it so unique.

To truly understand the development of jazz, we would need to take ourselves back to New Orleans in the early 1900s (or is it the late 1800s?), watch the musicians, or walk alongside the marching bands. Different jazz styles may have evolved since, but I strongly suspect that if we could hear music in New Orleans well before the turn of the twentieth century, we would recognize much of it as jazz.

I think, in response to the question "Who was the first jazz musician?", bassist and journalist Philip Booth sums it up when he says, "someone from NOLA."

# CHAPTER 2

## *The music*

### DEFINING JAZZ

MANY PEOPLE EXPERIENCE a time when they hear music that has such a profound effect on them they spend the rest of their life exploring and investigating that moment. For some people, that music is jazz.

So what makes jazz different from other music, and what are its characteristics? With such a mixed and vibrant heritage, you might think it would be challenging to describe jazz. Yet, that diverse heritage gives jazz its identifying characteristics.

Most musicians could arrange a set of notes to create a tune. But what makes one set of notes classical, another folk, and another jazz? It is not just the arrangement and order of the notes but the playing style: the emphasis, subtle holds or delayed entries, the energy, emotion, whether the tempo is adhered to or not.

### INSTRUCTIONS VS IMPROVISATION

WRITTEN MUSIC IS a series of instructions. Using universally understood conventions helps the composer convey instructions to musicians. A series of marks, lines, clefs, and positions on a stave denotes pitch, and different annotations dictate patterns, keys, and rhythms. Additional instructions may be added, such as *allegro*, *largo*, *diminuendo*, or *fortissimo*, which mean "go quickly," "slow and dignified," "gradually get quieter" or "play strongly," respectively. The instructions guide musicians, and the styles and patterns create a type of music. While there is some freedom of interpretation, the instructions largely come from the composer's mind to those playing. In theory, this means a composer who lived decades ago can control how musicians play their music today. People may rewrite sections and include new instruments and harmonies—these are arrangements of that music—but largely the music of Handel, Bach, Beethoven, Prokofiev, and hundreds of other composers is played similarly today as it was at its debut.

Now, think another way. Decide a concept, an idea, and give this to a collective. Let them determine parameters—maybe a chord series or key changes. There may be an outline with volume, tempo, instrumentation, and spaces left for solos. The spaces (rests) may be a set number of bars—twelve, twenty-four, thirty-two—or it might be left to the musician to decide. This is a simplified concept of jazz music. The ideas will be translated according to the musicians playing, their instruments, and the mood. It is a collective way of playing, so each musician listens to the others and may add harmonies, come in, fade out, respond, or lead. Usually, the rhythm section (drums, piano, bass, banjo) provides a beat, and against this, other instruments play melodies or improvise around the offbeats and misplaced accents. Of course, musicians from the rhythm section can perform solos too.

So, jazz is music played in a certain way. Does this help? I hope so, but we should go deeper. In jazz music, the accent is on the weaker or "off" beats. This creates a "swing" or "bounce." Next, add syncopation—different rhythm patterns to create texture, harmonies, and disharmonies. Syncopation adds richness, timbre, and energy. An example of syncopation occurs when a rhythm pattern is divided unevenly. For instance, in an eight-beat pattern, the rhythm, each bar, instead of being divided evenly into 4/4 plus 4/4, or 2/4 plus 2/4 plus 2/4 plus 2/4, it is perhaps 3/4 and 3/4 plus 2/4. Syncopation is the essence of jazz, but composers have used it for centuries, and it is found in Western, African, and Asian music. In any music, chords flow and sequences of notes create melodies, but jazz has added "color" produced by using extra notes to give texture, *glissandos* (slides) added (by the composer or player) or perhaps dissonant tones to energize the music and add complexity.

There may be overlapping rhythms (polyrhythms), so a 32-beat melody (such as "Frère Jacques") can be in 8/4 and the accompaniment in 4/8 (both create a total of 32 beats—the 8/4 repeated four times and the 4/8 repeated eight times). Counterpoint can add additional complexity—this is where two tunes are independent of each other in one way (e.g. harmony) yet follow the same melody or key changes, so there is a relationship between them. Put some or all of these elements together with improvisation, and you are playing, or hearing, jazz.

Forget the old hat notion notion that jazz is for unskilled musicians. It is challenging to weave complex rhythmic patterns together without just creating noise. To create music, there must be an understanding of what is good to hear and not. Musicians need to know their instrument, its tuning, and how they intend to play.

They need to:

- question whether their ideas will fit with the rest of what is happening
- work out harmonies
- know scales, tempo, rhythm patterns
- be able to listen and hear those around them, as well as their own sound—to react and know precisely when to stop playing or when to step in
- play and stay in tune, and pick precisely the right note to create a dissonant sound for emphasis or atmosphere.

Any musician can try to play jazz, but some will just make "jazz-like" noises. They are not playing jazz until they feel it.

Among the worst musical "sins" is when people "jazz up" numbers by adding a swing to the beat or trying to play jazz like a classical musician. If musicians want to play jazz, they have to play jazz, not a "jazzy" version of another genre.

Jazz is based on improvisation. Give a piece to three jazz musicians, and each will play it a different way, or more likely, start working together to create something new. More than any other genre, jazz requires the instrument to be an extension of the player, because with its improvisational aspects, it relies on the musician's character. Ultimately, the character of the player makes one different from another.

A composer cannot be too precious about their score because jazz musicians will each interpret their nugget of an idea differently. Improvisation is important, but a good player uses their ear and knowledge of harmony to ensure they never lose control of the musical idea or where they are going.

Elements of jazz are the same as any music. Chords, melodies, themes, motifs (decorative sequences), riffs (repeated sequences), and instruments are played similarly to other genres. It is how the elements are put together that makes jazz different.

Knowing their instruments means many jazz musicians can play in extended ranges (like the *altissimo* range on the tenor saxophone) and use their instruments in different ways (creating percussive sounds on the body of the double bass, for example). However—and this is a point made by many musicians—there are rules. All musicians have to play within parameters and there has to be familiarity that a listener can feel, something linking passages that the ear can follow.

## STRUCTURE AND COMPOSITION

GENERALLY, A JAZZ number has three parts. The melody (A) opens the number and may be repeated. The middle section (B) is based on improvisation, often around an agreed concept, and a return to the melody closes. This AABA is the simplest structure. Jazz numbers also use the ABBA structure, where the middle section includes two improvised sections—perhaps played by different soloists. The structure can vary—sometimes at the time it is being played! The call and response may be used where a musician responds to the melody by improvising around it or repeating it differently (e.g. changing the key). Different meters can be introduced to overlap and create textures and layers.

In free-form jazz, the composition is spontaneous. The group improvises, using concepts to return to. They may never form a recognizable "tune," but good free-form players play sounds that work together.

---

### Blue notes

Blue notes are the notes between notes we hear. We know they are there, but it isn't easy to write them in because our way of writing music down does not allow it. Think of "Frère Jacques" again: the first three notes rise in equal intervals, but if you slide up to each one, you are hitting other notes, only just discernible to our ears. These are essentially notes between or just below the tone (flattened). It is usually easier for a singer than an instrumentalist to demonstrate this, but a musician can use *glissando* (such as a trombonist sliding up to a note) to introduce blue notes, and a pianist can add them as trills. These blue notes regularly feature in blues (and less often in jazz) to add a bluesy feel. Musicians find those notes and use them to color their music. They can be played fast and used for comedic effect, or they can be played long and slow for a sad, melancholy feel.

---

Jazz can include complex key changes and rhythm patterns, but listeners find comfort when the music returns to a familiar melody or previously heard pattern. This is called the "return." Returns are also used to segue into a different number (or even genre).

Modern jazz uses a broader range of instruments than ever. Many of these instruments play notes across a tone, like a tabla with its resonant, full-bodied "whomp." To explain, semitones are divided, in theory, into cents (one-hundredths). For example, between, say, B flat and B, or F and F sharp, there are 100 cents. The human ear can detect changes of around five cents, so, between B flat and B, we could potentially detect twenty note changes in what we currently hear as a semitone. Instruments such as the sitar, oud, zummāra, and bandura have different tunings. They play notes between semitones—or some of them—so, along with the development of electronic amplifiers and instruments, expanding the instruments used in jazz opens up a world of different sound combinations.

All this said, jazz's engaging accents and intimations cannot be taught. A player may understand harmonics, technicalities, keys, scales, and all the music theories, but they may not be a good jazz musician. You can teach someone harmonics, dissonance, or demonstrate syncopation by setting it up against a steady beat from the rhythm section, but you cannot teach the subtlety involved in shifting melodic emphasis or shaping the music to create sonic pictures. Beyond technicalities, a player relies on their sensitivity to the true nature of the music—they have to let it "take them" and feel it.

If you have found listening to jazz difficult, you may never have heard the right players. Audiences treated to master jazz musicians such as Wynton Marsalis, Courtney Pine, Mats Gustafsson, Nubya Garcia, Zoe Rahman, or Leo Pellegrino find listening to jazz a doddle. As Miles Davis once said, "Good music is good music, no matter what kind of music it is."

And that is another point. Nearly all music created is dreadful, whether it is jazz, classical, folk, or any other kind. Most music ever composed by students or great composers is lousy. Occasionally, something good is created. Something that will be respected, loved, and played by others. The creation of any good music is part of a long process during which, in most cases, a lot of bad music precedes the good stuff. I say this to explain that what we like as listeners, to us, is good music, but in reality, you don't need to understand any of what I have described above. If you hear good music, you know it. If you like it, you like it. That's it. If it happens to be jazz, you like jazz.

## IMPROVISATION

THE DIFFERENCE BETWEEN improvised and composed music is the latter is written down. In jazz, musicians may compose on the spot then dissect and rework the music. Today's jazz bears only a passing resemblance to the music that originated in America's Deep South, because bebop, free jazz, fusion, or the profoundly explorative jazz music of the twenty-first century was still to come. Early jazz recordings would be unrecognizable to some of today's jazz lovers. Yet, there are enough shared characteristics to make the new and old music jazz. The musicians have changed little in character, apart from their social awareness and their use of technology. The desire to connect with others, reflect social change, and share musical ideas is the same whether the player is from the turn of the twentieth century, the mid-1960s, or today.

While New Orleans remains the heart of traditional jazz, you can also hear it blended with hip hop, R&B, garage, and folk. A walk down New Orleans' Bourbon Street on an early evening will take you through every decade of jazz. You may see loud, exciting street bands like the Slow Rollas or catch snippets of fusion music coming from the doorways of clubs and cafés. When I was last in New Orleans, I heard a beautiful voice in the distance and followed the sound. It led me to Alicia Renée, aka "Blue Eyes"—a singer who has performed across the globe—performing to a small crowd on a corner near Frenchmen Street in the Faubourg Marigny. Jazz is everywhere, still, in the city it came from. However you look at it, jazz is one part of the universal language of music, with its own way of speaking—and it is a way more and more people are coming to understand.

## COMBINATIONS

As JAZZ MUSIC spread, several things had happened in the preceding decades, making it easier and helping increase the depth of music played. The saxophone had been invented in 1846 by Adolphe Sax, but few had made it to America until the 1900s. After this, the saxophone became associated with jazz, adding versatility and a vast range of sounds. Since the late 1930s, the addition of valves to brass instruments, such as the French horn and trumpet, has made them far more versatile. In early music, the bass brass instrument was the weirdly shaped and heavy serpent, but in the late nineteenth century, the valved, portable tuba replaced it. So, with valved instruments and portable brass, a jazz band could offer everything from delicate semi-voiced notes to deep, thunking foghorn-like blasts. Today, new technology and variations on keyboards and percussive sounds add more possibilities to jazz's toolbox.

There is no set "orchestration" for a jazz ensemble. There can be any number of players and instruments—it depends on the sound they want to create. Many jazz musicians in the past played more than one instrument. Press photographs of early jazz musicians often show the group, say a quintet, and in front of the drums would be a dozen instruments to demonstrate this versatility. Today, this still applies. I recently watched the six-strong wind section of the Down for the Count Swing Orchestra as they switched from saxophones to flutes to piccolos, with two of the players also playing clarinets.

So the question "What is jazz?" can be answered partly by saying it is music incorporating a swung beat, syncopated rhythms, and improvisation. Too simple? Of course, but really, who wants to define and limit jazz? If you ask musicians to define jazz, they tend to ask "Why?" Many dislike the perceived limitations of labels in any case. If someone is called a jazz musician, do they only play jazz? Of course not. Most musicians are just that—musicians.

# JAZZ AND OTHER GENRES

JAZZ IS A great connector, providing links to other genres and influenced by them. Charles Mingus was influenced by gospel, Duke Ellington, Debussy, and Ravel. Cecil Taylor was inspired by Stravinsky, Bartok, and Austrian composer Anton Webern. Hip hop, reggae, and funk have jazz references. The jazz-rock music of Jimi Hendrix and Frank Zappa relied on jazz rhythms and syncopation.

From classical composers to punk bands, musicians have borrowed jazz riffs, patterns, and beats. For their part, other genres give jazz musicians ideas about phrasing and notation. Musicians acknowledge this. Jazz bassist John Edwards and saxophonist and composer Mats Gustafsson told me they grew up liking punk music. Musicians such as John Lydon (Sex Pistols) and Elvis Costello like jazz and countless other popular artists have their roots in jazz.

Courtney Pine, Shabaka Hutchings, Jamie Cullum, Jools Holland, and Leo Pellegrino (To Many Zooz) have done much to popularize jazz, with music that encapsulates rhythm, familiar popular tunes, and jazz essences that appeal to modern audiences.

Musicians including Adele, Alison Moyet, Lady Gaga, and Annie Lennox have recorded and performed jazz numbers. Many of their original compositions have jazz references (Adele's "Rolling in the Deep" (Columbia 2010), for example). On his last CD, *Blackstar* (Iso/Columbia 2016), the late David Bowie used a jazz quartet (saxophonist Donny McCaslin, guitarist Ben Monder, drummer Mark Guiliana, and keyboard player Jason Linder) as principal musicians.

Young people love this new, energized mix of amazing sounds. Bands such as Polar Bear, Moon Hooch, Sons of Kemet, and Dinosaur have switched young people on to jazz—providing a modern take with electronic effects, different takes on standards, and original compositions. Players show the world the wonders of jazz, given a modern twist. Leo Pellegrino astounded the audience at the Royal Albert Hall, London, when he played "Moanin'" at a Mingus Promenade concert, dancing with his baritone, adding cheeky bum wiggles, and generally having a good time playing. The audience drank it in.

## JAZZ AND CLASSICAL MUSIC

I MENTIONED CLASSICAL composers earlier, but it is worth diving deeper into the inextricable links between jazz and classical music. Claude Debussy used the pentatonic (five notes to an octave) scale so often used in jazz music. His music included disharmonic chords, unresolved sequences, and sudden switches into different keys (modulations). Along with also using the whole tone scale (six equal intervals in a scale), Debussy's music inspired jazz musicians, including Thelonious Monk and Bix Beiderbecke. Debussy used one of the most common jazz rhythms—the short-long-short note sequences in his "Golliwog's Cakewalk," and jazz musicians have referenced his music. Australian pianist Rory Clark points out, "Bill Evans brought the classical lyricism of Debussy to jazz piano plus contrapuntal lines and melodies."

In the 1920s and '30s, there was a brief period when jazz was popular in the Soviet Union, (until the government discouraged this "bourgeois" music). Shostakovich's Suite for Jazz Orchestra No. 2 (later nicknamed "The Jazz Suite") was written in 1938 for Victor Knushevitsky's State Jazz Orchestra. Victor was the brother of the renowned cellist Sviatoslav Knushevitsky. The suite was written as a classical score, but it includes jazz influences. Incidentally, the score was "lost" until 1999, when three movements, the "Scherzo," "Lullaby," and "Serenade" were orchestrated by British composer and arranger Gerard McBurney, and premiered at the Henry Wood London Promenade concerts in 2000.

Stravinsky was Russian but moved to France, then became an American citizen. His *Soldier's Tale* of 1918 contains jazz elements, and his *Ragtime for Eleven Instruments* (1918) and *Piano Rag Music* (1919) included jazz rhythms and tempos. In America, he was enchanted by Woody Herman's orchestra and in 1945 wrote his *Ebony Concerto* for Herman, and the clarinetist and his orchestra premiered it. Although known as an American classical composer, Aaron Copland uses blue notes in his 1926 Piano Concerto, which was inevitably and affectionately called "The Jazz Concerto."

## JAZZ IN EUROPE

IN FRANCE, JAZZ was taken seriously from the early 1900s. The Quintet du Hot Club de France began in the 1930s and featured French-gypsy guitarist Django Reinhardt, who combined jazz and gypsy musical styles with such success he became the first non-American to influence jazz players. His fellow performer at the club was one of the world's finest jazz violinists—Stephane Grappelli.

Maurice Ravel admired Gershwin's music and was keen to learn jazz techniques such as transitioning key changes and rhythm patterns. His Piano Concerto for the Left Hand and his Piano Concerto in G Major have jazz influences.

Many were unsure about adapting jazz to a concert setting. American composers concentrated on classical works and popular songs, but in Europe, artists such as the German composer Paul Hindemith wrote pieces for orchestra with jazz references. Jazz and blues found their way into several compositions of European composers, such as Darius Milhaud's ballet *La Creation du Monde*. However, some American composers realized the popularity of jazz. Aaron Copland wrote jazz effects into his works, including *Music for the Theatre* in 1925 and, over twenty years later, in 1947, *Concerto for Clarinet, Strings and Harp*. Morton Gould wrote *Boogie-Woogie Etude* for piano in 1943, and Mark-Anthony Turnage and John Scofield wrote *Scorched* (for jazz trio and orchestra) in 2001.

George Gershwin became an influential classical composer who used jazz influences extensively, and he was entranced by the rhythm patterns found in jazz. His first major work was *Rhapsody in Blue*, which was commissioned by bandleader Paul Whiteman in 1924. Introduced by its instantly recognizable upward-sweeping chords, the rhapsody proved a popular piece, and *An American in Paris* followed in 1928. Both use blues melodies, jazz rhythms, and patterns, with instrumentation primarily using wind instruments. Gershwin's opera *Porgy and Bess* (1934) was a masterpiece and featured a cast of classically trained Africa-American singers. Classical in nature but unmistakably jazz-influenced, the work remains popular, and the aria "Summertime" is the most recorded jazz standard.

Once they realized jazz's potential, American classical and non-classical composers wrote works based on it. Examples are Ellington's *Black, Brown and Beige* (1943), *Harlem* (1950), and *Deep South Suite* (1947). In 1959, Howard Brubeck's "Dialogue for Jazz Combo and Orchestra" was premiered by the New York Philharmonic Orchestra and featured his brother Dave's jazz quartet improvising against the orchestra. John Henry Lewis wrote music for the Modern Jazz Quartet and symphony orchestra. Other classical compositions influenced by jazz include Malcolm Arnold's Concerto No. 2 for Clarinet and Orchestra (1974), Michael Tippett's Symphony No. 3 (1972), and more composers linked the genres, including Rolf Liebermann, Leonard Bernstein, Gunther Schuller, Richard Rodney Bennett, and John Dankworth.

## THE BEAUTIFUL THIRD STREAM

THERE ARE PLACES in music where jazz and classical compositions come so close they almost touch, with scores containing both written and improvised sections. Conductor, composer, author, and historian Gunther Schuller first coined the term "third stream," and its exponents included Jimmy Guiffre, Darius Milhaud, and Schuller himself (*Transformation* 1956). It is music that cannot be defined as classical or jazz, where jazz lends elements to classical and vice versa.

Third-stream music includes some memorable works because it satisfies the structures that appeal to classical music lovers while incorporating the swing and sassiness that appeal to jazz audiences. An example is Gershwin's previously mentioned *Rhapsody in Blue*. The strings' sweeping harmonic rises and falls, and the piece's symphonic orchestration, align with classical music. Yet, there are also intrinsic patterns in the composition that align it with jazz. The term "third stream" allows for a definition that describes music with jazz or classical influences, while acknowledging it is neither. It is just another label. If there is a disagreement over whether a piece of music is classical or jazz, calling it third stream resolves the problem.

## APPLYING JAZZ THEORY TO CLASSICAL MUSIC

NO ONE HAS yet wholly unraveled the characteristics of jazz, but composer, jazz pianist, and theorist George Russell applied jazz theory to classical music. His compositions included parts for soloists including Bill Evans, John Coltrane, and Paul Bley. Before Russell, music theory was reserved for classical studies, and even musicians were unsure of the rules that applied to jazz. Russell analyzed jazz, wrote rules, explained them, and several publications incorporated his jazz theories, which was significant because it gave jazz acceptance and respect among academics. Works such as *Living Time* (Columbia 1972) and *The London Concert* (Label Bleu 1990), where Russell recorded with Bill Evans and The Living Time Orchestra, respectively, proved popular.

Modern jazz musicians, including Mats Gustafsson, compose pieces for orchestra. Gustafsson's compositions include *Back - or For-word* (1989), a chamber piece for cello, piano, reeds, percussion, voice, video, and performance artist, and *Bortviska* (1989), for large ensembles and conductor.

> Today, composers, including Yves Leveille and Anders Koppel, continue the "third-stream approach," which combines classical arrangements with jazz in their compositions—they create incredibly emotive music. I asked Leveille what writing this music means for him. He said:
>
> "For me, it's a natural and organic process, especially in this day and age where almost every genre of music rubs shoulders and influences each other in a more natural way than we think.
>
> "I have always liked to take care of the writing of my music, dig the possibilities, and reach a second level, which allows music to find its own personality through all possible influences. I have always proceeded in this way, and it was confirmed during my studies in writing classical/contemporary music.

> "Jazz brings a freshness and spontaneity to the music via improvisation—the rhythms, the harmonies, and more. Reaching a level of excellence in jazz requires rigorous and long-term work, so for me, it is much the same as creating a classical piece of music. There are common areas in both schools; you just have to permit yourself to explore openly.
>
> "What I also find interesting during the concert performances of my pieces is that, finally, the music has its own identity, personality, and definition because of the writing. Having windows for improvisation means the music subtly changes, redefines itself, improves, and when the magic happens, it becomes really interesting. You can't get bored!"

Jazz-based compositions included in the repertoires of internationally known orchestras gained credibility and respect for the genre and brought it to the attention of classical audiences. While differences in modal changes, rhythms, and instrumentation distinguish the jazz and classical genres, much joins them too.

As well as classical music, many musicians incorporate jazz into R&B, hip hop, garage, folk, and rock. Every person who listens to popular music of any kind today has probably heard a rhythm based on jazz.

## GENRE-HOPPING AND COLLABORATIONS

THE LINKS BETWEEN jazz and other genres are emphasized when musicians seamlessly genre-hop. On his 2016 album *Nonagram* (Soweto 2016), saxophonist Soweto Kinch touches on blues, street poetry, funk, free improvisation, and street music. Shabaka Hutchins, part of the new wave of jazz, brings reggae, calypso, hip hop, and, of course, jazz to his music. Many young musicians include references to masters of the past, but they also have individual takes on the music. This gains them both respect with traditionalists while bringing in new listeners.

Nowadays, with all the discussions on linking jazz and other genres, and whether jazz is a separate genre, largely resolved, young musicians who really could not care less about labels are linking jazz to other genres and attracting a whole new audience. Elliot Galvin, Laura Jurd, Mike Casey, Nubya Garcia, Melissa Aldana, Mary Halvorson, Melody Gardot, Moses Boyd, Kit Downes, and Cécile McLorin Salvant, to mention a few, are tuned into the kind of music their peers want to see and hear, but they also create new music with jazz as its root.

Artists such as composer and musician John Zorn collaborate with young people. The Spike Orchestra, led by Sam Eastmond and Nikki Franklin, plays jazz-based music, which Zorn composes, and their albums reach a broad audience. In 2021, Cafe OTO premiered some Zorn pieces in London, with Eastmond conducting the National Youth Jazz Orchestra as part of the London Jazz Festival. Watching the expressions on the faces of the audience as the young musicians demonstrated their talents and understanding of the music was a delight. The arrangements, at times, could have fitted a classical setting, but here—linked to Klezmer rhythm and with jazz elements infused throughout—it sat very neatly in a place between symphonic music and jazz.

Divisions between genres are necessary to market, place, and describe music, but where they mingle and mix can be found soundscapes of incredible beauty and wonder.

## JAZZ AND OTHER GENRES

JAZZ WAS NOT yet around when classical composers, including Beethoven, Mozart, and Wagner, were at the height of their creativity, but if it had been, I would wager it would have found its way into their music.

With syncopation, swung beat, and sexiness, jazz lends itself to any genre, and because previous genres influenced jazz, listeners find a whisper of the familiar and a subliminal connection to their own culture.

We should take a moment here to appreciate the significant impact of jazz over a relatively short timescale. Classical, folk, and hymns, have been around for centuries. At this point, jazz (officially) has just been around for over a century, yet it has had more influence than any other style on the music we hear today—from Latin to reggae, pop, rock, funk, and hip hop. If it were not for jazz, these other genres would be nowhere near as sophisticated as they are now.

Jazz has had such a massive impact on music firstly because it is different. Its rhythms and multicultural, poly-anthropological origins spoke to people of all colors, cultures, and creeds. From the beginning, it did not sound like any other music.

Secondly, because it was unlike any other music, it was not "owned" by any culture or nation. It provided a focus for people whose identity had been stripped away or those who felt disenchanted with America. Enslaved people were growing apart from their own culture in a land with different expectations, values, and views on the value of a human life, and discrimination against them was tangible. Jazz helped these mixed, separated peoples establish a new heritage, and it united people who were disconnected from their own cultures. These people now had a base, a music that was theirs.

Thirdly, jazz fills "vacuum" areas. It is hard to explain, but when you hear music, there are moments you feel totally immersed in it. The music completely takes you, and no other music finds this "sweet spot" so often as jazz. Classical music can have elements that take you somewhere else. It lifts and presses emotional buttons. Oratorio can express emotions, put feelings into words—not your words but words that can be powerful. Folk music tells stories; Klezmer is moving and musical; rock is exciting. Music pushes many buttons, but there is always a part missing—a slight vacuum. Jazz slots sweetly into the breach. It is emotional, angry, sweet, harsh, and it takes you to another place. It grounds, excites, and comforts—it does all these things like no other genre. Improvisation allows more emotion, more pull and push, and more variation. Jazz is the music chosen to establish an atmosphere, provide a backdrop or a message. It comprises so many parts that any new genre can borrow from jazz and enfold elements from it. Scat singing transfers to rap, the rhythm section transfers to bass lines, and drum beats to rock and roll. Different genres borrow elements from jazz, but these elements are only together as a whole in jazz itself.

No music has taken to the worldwide stage the way jazz has. It comes down to jazz's ability to be infused into other cultures and have them infuse into it. I am not talking necessarily about traditional jazz but jazz in its many forms. Jazz in China is jazz with a Chinese feel; jazz in Prague has a Czech touch; French jazz has a *je ne sais quoi*. Each scene is unique, but jazz is still jazz with a swung beat and syncopation—yet the subtle infusions from each culture make it unique in each area.

When I discussed how much jazz had influenced other types of music with artists, they agreed. Saxophonist, composer, and conductor Phil Meadows said, "Developing the skill set of a jazz musician allows you to connect with all genres of music. Its creativity, spontaneity, and openness to adaptation and collaboration are what make it both intangible and magical."

Songwriter and producer Luther McGinnis adds, "Jazz intersects with soul and black gospel," while Deelee Dubé commented, "Marvin Gaye (during his Motown days) delivered some interpretations of jazz and Latin standards, as did Michael Jackson when he sang 'Happy' (the love theme from *Lady Sings the Blues*)."

I wrote earlier about how jazz imbibes local cultures. An excellent study of this is found in a paper written by musician Fergus Hall, titled "Making Connections: The Influence of Scottish Traditional Music in Contemporary Scottish Jazz." In his paper, Hall says:

*For some decades now, jazz musicians from other European countries have been drawing on their cultural heritage as a means of expanding and developing jazz as an art form. Perhaps the most recognised, or at least the most discussed instance of the exploration of intersections between jazz and native traditional music, is in Scandinavia... Native traditional music allowed*

*Scandinavian jazz music to assume a role separate from its defined American origins. Instead, it creates music that takes on a level of "semantic potentiality" that is "relevant to performers and audiences" (Bjerstedt 2015). The earliest instance of this on record is the seminal album Jazz på svenska (Johansson 1964) by Swedish pianist Jan Johansson. While substantial jazz elements remained like improvisation, the overtly Swedish aesthetic derived from Swedish traditional music demonstrates how a sense of ownership of the music was being established... Evidently, this "meaning" was not to be found in a defined American style of jazz but rather a style that could develop in a way that reflected the cultural backgrounds and issues of those in whose hands the music now found itself.*

## CHINA

SIMILAR FINDINGS CONCLUDE that jazz is "tweaked" according to its location. For example, during the 1920s, due to a the rise of cultural exchange between the East and West, China's jazz scene became the domain of wealthy patrons in clubs listening to Western jazz music. Chinese jazz arrangers either translated standards into Mandarin or used oriental instruments in jazz numbers, either way adding a Chinese feel. During the 1940s, the Jimmy King Jazz Band was the main all-Chinese jazz band. In 1949, the Cultural Revolution ironically saw the banning of jazz and other Western music. Jazz was considered crude, dirty, and even compared to pornography. It was not until the 1980s that China again welcomed musicians from all over the world. Of course, it was much more complex than this, but in a nutshell, jazz was popular, then banned, and now it is popular again, and American and European musicians play Chinese composers' music, so the exchange is two-way.

In 2006, jazz music education cooperation began between Chinese and American music colleges. The rise of the internet allowed more musicians to post their music online, and the cultural exchange continues. In 2015, Blue Note established a venue in Beijing, and there is now Blue Note Shanghai. Films such as *Crazy Rich Asians* (Warner 2018) have seen jazz become fashionable, now being called "hot" jazz in China. Taipei has had a Blue Note venue since 1974 and a thriving jazz scene. Hopefully, China will remain open to new and exciting music, including jazz—and that it also gives jazz some elements of its distinctive music.

# INDIA

INDIA HAS A thriving jazz scene. From the 1920s, African-American musicians brought jazz to the subcontinent. They fused Indian classical music (which already had elements of improvisation) and jazz for film scores in the Hindi film industry, and later in Bollywood productions. From the 1930s until the 1950s, interest grew, with artists including Chris Perry and Rudy Cotton performing to enthusiastic audiences. Jazz provided a meeting point for musicians from India's diverse cultures and religions. Goans, Anglo-Indians, Parsi, and Hindu communities found a commonality in jazz. This collaboration of Indian classical musicians with jazz musicians led to Indo-jazz, which Ravi Shankar, Yusef Lateef, Joe Harriott, John McLaughlin, and other jazz musicians pioneered. Elements of Indo-jazz strongly influenced free jazz. The Piano Man Jazz Club in New Delhi, Shisha Jazz Café in Puna, and Windmills Craftworks in Bangalore attract consistent crowds today. The Delhi International Jazz and Blues Festival and Jodhpur Riff attract artists from across the world as well as Indian artists, including Varijashree Venugopal, Rhythm Shaw, Time Wise, and Gino Banks.

## OTHER PLACES

IN ECUADOR, JAZZ regularly appears in the programs of several venues, including the famous El Pobre Diablo club in Quito and the Teatro Sucre in the old town center, which host visiting US and European jazz stars. The Quito jazz festival hosts acts from across the globe, and when I was there, I saw acts from Canada, Spain, and other South American countries. Columbia has a thriving jazz scene, and Bogota clubs have hosted musicians from Europe, including Mats Gustafsson.

Jazz continues to grow and develop, and never loses its connection to its origins. It feels incredibly positive as old works with new, different ideas appear and are included.

Most musicians I have spoken to describe jazz as a visionary-filled genre, a sharing of community, experiences, and without boundaries—a genre that allows musicians freedom to express themselves through the music.

It is a mistake, though, to talk of any scene—whether it be the UK, Europe, Asia, or the Middle East—as coming about spontaneously and having no bearing on each other. None of the global scenes would have come about without the American development of jazz music as a genre.

Musical taste is a personal choice, and obviously not everyone appreciates jazz. And this is absolutely fine.

One musician put his finger on it when he commented, "Why do so many people think they don't like 'jazz' when they hear the word but then like the music when they hear it? I once had a reviewer say, 'I f***g hate jazz, but I like this'!"

Writer/producer John Farley told me, "I was doing a jazz gig in a club back in the day. One night, I put Coltrane's *Transition* on the system, and the owner made me take it off."

Bassist/composer/educator Rick McLaughlin said, "Coming back from a commercial break, host David Letterman excoriated Paul Schaffer (Letterman's musical director and bandleader) with, 'What the hell was that?' It was the band playing 'Giant Steps.'"

Just before a performance—the instruments and stage are ready.

Photo credit: Luciano Rossetti

# CHAPTER 3

## *Game changers*

THERE ARE PEOPLE whose influence has been so profound that jazz was not the same after them—whose approach is entirely different or whose actions challenge accepted parameters. They are not always musicians. Some record label bosses, entrepreneurs, and managers instigated profound changes. They may not always be the first names to come to mind, and it sometimes takes a deeper study to reveal that, without them, music, and jazz in particular, would not be as rich or diverse as it is today.

## THE BEFORE AND AFTER PEOPLE

THE MORE I learn, the more I understand that each individual puts something unique on the table. Sometimes it is a small step with long-term ramifications; other times, it is a profoundly different approach that makes people rethink. The game changers include those who have bucked tradition, spoken out against injustice, and laid down societal challenges for the music industry.

In no particular order, we will go through my shortlist of artists who I think changed and enriched the jazz scene more than most. I shall explain my picks and then hand over to musicians who gave their own choices. There are, of course, more recent game changers too, but it isn't easy to gauge their final influences because their body of work is still ongoing.

### RONNIE SCOTT AND HIS ASSOCIATES

SAXOPHONIST AND ENTREPRENEUR Ronnie Scott helped establish the UK as one of the world's great centers for jazz. Scott set up a small club in London whose success was impacted partly due to arcane attitudes in the UK regarding music and dancing, and partly because of a Musicians' Union dispute between the UK and US, which made it extremely difficult for musicians to cross the Atlantic to play.

Scott and his associates—including singer George Melly and trumpeter Humphrey Lyttleton—became part of the "bottle club" scene in London. Bottle clubs took place in basements beneath retail premises in districts around Soho. Musicians who could not find work in the theaters of the West End would migrate to Soho during the evenings and find a bottle club to play at and maybe drink. The austerity that prevailed after the Second World War provided few chances for men and women to dance and drink together. However, in bottle clubs, people could dance, listen to the few well-worn jazz records from America they still had, and play—highly nefarious activities in austerity-ridden Britain in the 1950s. The jazz played in bottle clubs was nothing like the jazz of swing bands that played on television shows and in West End venues. Scott hosted one bottle club and he wanted to expand to a full-blown jazz club.

In the 1940s, the Musicians' Union in the UK and the American Federation of Musicians fell out over performance rights, recording issues, and many other factors. The disagreement led to a decline in creativity in the newly emerged bebop scene, which Scott found frustrating. This state of affairs was a game-changing occurrence in itself. It inadvertently led to the UK and European scenes diversifying and growing away from the American one, which some would argue benefited jazz long term. However, it was detrimental to any transatlantic cooperation.

Centered in Harlem, bebop—a fast, solo-led jazz style with rapid changes, requiring technical excellence—had changed how people viewed jazz. However, the chances of hearing it outside America was limited as US bebop musicians weren't coming to the UK. The wranglings went on for years.

In 1949, attempts to bring Benny Goodman to play the London Palladium as part of a variety show were thwarted when the Musicians' Union insisted that the Palladium's resident players replaced Goodman's American musicians. Nat King Cole came to the Palladium but could not use his American musicians, even when British musicians joined them as support. The union banned clarinet player Sidney Bechet and saxophonist Coleman Hawkins from playing in the UK. A few promoters arranged for American guest musicians to appear unannounced and duly received fines under the ancient 1920 Aliens Order.

In 1947, Scott, aware that incredible changes were going on in America, went on a liner to hear the music for himself. He knew he wanted to bring this energy to the UK and could get nothing like this jazz in the backrooms of pubs, semi-legal cellars, and tacky dance halls. Scott and others regularly found work on liners for a few years, playing background jazz for clients on transatlantic crossings. When they docked in America, they went to clubs and experienced as much music as possible. Stan Tracey, later Scott's in-house pianist from 1960 to 1967, spent six months working the boats in the early 1950s. The pay was dire, but it meant that he could sit in clubs like the famed Birdland, soaking up the music of Parker, Gillespie, and others.

In London, Scott highlighted the absurdity of the unions' dispute. His band was playing at the Windmill Theatre one evening in the mid-1950s, and the spotlight fell upon Sidney Bechet, who was in the audience. Fortunately, he had his clarinet with him and played with Scott's band, effectively defying the ban. It resulted in a hefty fine for the organizers, but this small yet defiant act encouraged managers and musicians to defy the ban. Soon a lot of American players were playing in the UK, albeit unofficially, and venues were not getting fined.

Finally, an agreement was reached where US musicians could perform in the UK, provided British musicians played reciprocal gigs in America. Stan Tracey was a part of the early exchanges. As Dave Brubeck and Stan Kenton headlined concerts in the UK, Tracey began a week's residency in a New York jazz club. He started his one-hour set at 8 pm. What the club failed to tell him in advance was that the doors didn't open till 9 pm. Eventually, resolutions were found, and in 1956 Louis Armstrong came to the UK, followed by Dave Brubeck, Duke Ellington, Miles Davis, and others. These visits from jazz's great players gave the UK a powerful endorsement as a jazz destination and legitimized American musicians' careers outside America.

Scott and his business partner Pete King presented stellar musicians to a hungry audience at Ronnie Scott's Jazz Club on Gerrard Street. Scott arranged for English saxophonist Tubby Hayes to play New York's Half Note for a month's residency, and American saxophonist Zoot Sims played at Ronnie Scott's. Officially, this was the first time an American jazz musician had played in a British jazz club for almost thirty years (though not quite true unofficially).

Although time-wasting, the hiatus allowed the UK and US scenes to diverge along different pathways. Scott brought over traditional players and those pushing boundaries, such as Paul Bley. They played in Finsbury Park and other venues and, of course, Ronnie's jazz club, which could seat just ninety people and had no drinks license. Later, it moved to Frith Street, where it remains one of the key destinations for jazz lovers and musicians in the UK. Scott championed jazz at a time when stubbornness ruled. The union dispute was really about whether musicians were going to play live or be replaced by recordings.

## LOUIS ARMSTRONG

LOUIS ARMSTRONG PLAYED the cornet, then trumpet, with a different style and manner than anyone preceding him. He became the first global jazz superstar and was perhaps one of the first jazz artists to realize his worth, the impact his music could have, and the power he had to speak out on behalf of marginalized people. When he was sent out as a "jazz ambassador" by the American government to show the world how integrated America was, he could see the irony. Yet, rather than take on his government directly, Armstrong used jazz as a vehicle to highlight racial issues. He was sharp enough to know that changing just one word in the Andy Razaf/Harry Brooks/Fats Waller song "Black and Blue" would be enough to make a point—and it would be noticed.

After the lengthy fallout between the American Federation of Musicians and the UK's Musicians' Union in the 1950s, which resulted in no US and UK musicians crossing the Atlantic to play (legally at least) for several years, Armstrong was finally allowed to play in the UK. Apparently, he was asked if he would play an encore at a concert. Perhaps angry at the damage the disputes had caused, he is reported to have looked at his watch and said, "I am contracted to play for forty-five minutes, and I shall play for that, not a minute more, not a minute less." No encore ensued. He remained a popular, enigmatic musician and a strong supporter of civil rights. Armstrong used his power carefully, without alienating many people. He could raise issues but knew where the career-damaging line was.

## CHARLIE PARKER

MANY AGREE THAT Charlie Parker brought a breath of fresh air to jazz with his fiendishly fast playing, contrasting with the standardized deliveries up to that point. His bebop style introduced freedom for players, who have relished it ever since. He pioneered playing methods that are now part and parcel of jazz delivery. Searching for music he could hear but not play, Parker had several setbacks before finding his true path, and, ignoring criticism from those opposed to the new jazz, he forged his distinctive style. Despite his addiction to heroin, which led in part to his license to play in clubs being revoked for two years, he never gave up. Dying at the young age of thirty-four, Parker inspired others to "play what you hear." No one has ever played saxophone like Charlie Parker—or "Bird" as he is known.

## DUKE ELLINGTON

DUKE ELLINGTON CHANGED the paths of musicians in his bands, including Barney Bigard, Cootie Williams, Johnny Hodges, Harry Carney, Jimmy Blanton, and many more. He arranged pieces highlighting the strong parts of a soloist's technique and offered guidance. In his quiet way, he spoke against the accepted canons by creating music with profound spiritual and social messages that he deftly placed under the listening public's nose. He also wrote sacred works with classical lines, creating a bridge between one genre and another.

## LENNIE TRISTANO

PIANIST LENNIE TRISTANO was influenced by Charlie Parker, and he used dissonance and spontaneous solos in his works before they became popular playing styles. He recorded what was probably the first free jazz recordings (more on him in the free jazz section of this book), but his improvisation and approach to music influenced many who followed. He married the concept of playing complex rhythms over melodic lines—something many have tried to emulate. At the time, some of his techniques were experimental, such as overdubbing and using counterpoint in the left hand. Now, however, these are standard tools. Some of his recordings were considered so radical they were not released until after his death. There are accounts of Tristano inviting musicians to play in a studio and asking them to perform without instrumentation or instruction. Today, this is part of many studio sessions—seeing what happens. Tristano also inspired others, including Lee Konitz, probably his most famous student.

## IVY BENSON

IVY BENSON IS on my list because of her strength of character and how she stood up for women. Born in Leeds in the north of England, in 1913, Benson was a child prodigy, appearing as "Baby Benson" on the BBC aged just nine. In her teens, she played with Edna Croudson's Rhythm Girls sextet and stayed for six years before joining Teddy Joyce's band. She moved to London and formed The Ivy Benson Rhythm Girls, encouraged by bandleader and composer Jack Hylton. Benson invited female players she knew from the brass bands of north England and from popular combos to play in her band. In 1943, they got a twenty-two-week residency at the London Palladium before becoming BBC House Band in Bristol. Some male musicians felt outraged, and a delegation from the Musicians' Union met with the BBC to register their displeasure. Apart from the ever-supportive Jack Hylton and British dance bandleader Joe Loss, male bandleaders resented Benson. The critics were acerbic.

During the Second World War, Benson's ensembles played at military bases, which proved a good move, and they remained popular players of nostalgic and traditional numbers. Benson and her Rhythm Girls once again appeared at the Palladium and the Stoll Theatre (originally the London Opera House) in 1944. In 1945, Benson's authority as a bandleader gained public validation when Field Marshal Montgomery asked her and her band to play at the V-E Day celebrations in Berlin. In 1946, Benson took her band on a European tour with ENSA (Entertainment National Service Association). Several trips to Europe and the Middle East followed. Her band remained popular well into the 1980s. Benson navigated overt sexism in the UK in the early to mid-twentieth century and empowered female musicians. Several members of her band went on to have stellar careers, including drummer Crissy Lee.

## ORNETTE COLEMAN

ORNETTE COLEMAN IS included because he had the bravery, tenacity, and nous to ensure he had the right musicians around him, convincing them the time was right to unleash his version of free jazz to an unsuspecting audience at the Five Spot in 1959. Some critics were outraged, while others appreciated and enjoyed the new sound. Coleman made it okay for musicians to try new things, such as his two quartets recording *Free Jazz* (Atlantic 1961), where one quartet comes from each speaker, either sounding completely dissonant or working a treat, depending on your take.

## JOHN COLTRANE

JOHN COLTRANE CHANGED everything—the approach, the style, and the sound of jazz, along with how it was delivered. Nothing post-Coltrane is unaffected. He opened the door to new music with such power behind it. He combined secular with sacred, and his music has within it the anger against racism and discrimination, the despair at humanity's darkness, and the beauty of praise and worship. He faced the demons of his drug addiction and won; the music became more personal and beautiful. His modal technique paved the way for free jazz, yet his links to traditional jazz were strong, and his soul spoke through his music.

## ALBERT AYLER

ALBERT AYLER IS on my list for his truth-telling. His version of Gershwin's "Summertime" was a breakthrough moment when I understood how free jazz could tell a different story from the original track. In his incredible interpretation, Ayler says that a Negro slave mother putting her child to bed, singing a sweet song about a rich daddy and a good-looking mommy as depicted in the opera, was all rose-tinted nonsense. Ayler's version was more about the uncomfortable changes, the clashing notes, and the jarring disharmonies adding a fearful edge to the number—he was saying, "Look! This was how it was—fear, noise, and worry for the child." You can still hear Gershwin's composition in Ayler's version, but it is tempered with a truism that few deny. Truth was something Ayler brought to his music, from his inspired playing with trios and quartets, to his solo work, Ayler's abstract, spiritual style inspired many players who followed.

## MILES DAVIS

MILES DAVIS WAS a jazz chameleon. He fused jazz with rock and created something extraordinary. His reimagination of jazz music and understanding the importance of connection are outstanding. Not only that, he journeyed through different personas, becoming cool, modal, free, and rocky while retaining the essential Davis, as if these personas were a ruse to connect. His fusion performances resonated with young people, encouraging other jazz musicians. He created sound waves with his trumpet, which remain unmatched. He had a way of playing that became purer with time, and his intelligence and talent remain untouchable.

## HAZEL SCOTT

HAZEL SCOTT WAS a woman who withstood some of the harshest and targeted criticism. When she was just eight years old, Scott used to play piano to accompany ballet classes. Frank Damrosch, the founder of the Juilliard School, heard her playing Rachmaninoff's "Prelude in C Sharp Major" and was outraged because sixths were substituted for the ninth intervals. When he entered the room and saw a child was playing, he realized she had intuitively substituted the shorter interval because her hands were too small to span the gap between the notes for ninths. She was a genius. Damrosch gave her a special scholarship under his assistant dean's tutelage and care (she was eight years too young for an ordinary scholarship). The assistant dean, Oscar Wagner, taught her jazz techniques.

At thirteen, Scott joined her mother's jazz band, Alma Long Scott's American Creolians, and was given a spot playing piano at the Roseland Ballroom, following the Count Basie Orchestra. She instigated her own boogie-woogie style and proved a popular and engaging pianist. While her scholarship to the Juilliard School educated Scott in techniques, much of her musical education came from the jazz musicians, including Art Tatum, Lester Young, Fats Waller, and Billie Holiday, who visited her home.

At that time (1936), most jazz clubs—even the Cotton Club, where Duke Ellington and Cab Calloway headlined—were segregated, and it was rare for blacks and whites to share the stage. However, there were exceptions, notably Café Society in Sheridan Square, New York. Billie Holiday got Scott a spot at the club when Scott was just nineteen, and when Holiday left, Scott became the headline act. Her excellent piano playing, along with her sultry voice and beauty, made her a popular entertainer. The club became so popular that a second Café Society opened in an uptown neighborhood. Scott became a regular performer, and one performance so moved the president's wife,

Eleanor Roosevelt, that she asked to meet her after the show. Scott was still only twenty-two.

She married Adam Clayton Powell, the city's first African-American Congress candidate and for a while concentrated on being the wife of a politician and bringing up their son. She played concert halls and toured only when Powell was away. She became the first black woman to get a TV show—*The Hazel Scott Show*—on DuMont Television Network, and she became a highly respected musician. However, everything changed in 1950 when Scott's name appeared on a list of 151 people in the TV and radio industries who were suspected of being communist sympathizers in the McCarthy era. The list was called *Red Channels: The Report of Communist Influence in Radio and Television*. It was drawn up by *Counterattack*, a right-wing journal. It named actors, broadcasters, writers, and musicians who, according to its "sources," were manipulating the entertainment industry toward communist thinking. Unofficial but highly influential, the list got Scott blacklisted, and she was asked to appear before the House Un-American Activities Committee.

It was not surprising Scott's name appeared on a list—the list being more one of people who stirred up trouble than for those genuinely of communist persuasion. Café Society, where she had played, was, apparently, known to be a haunt of communist sympathizers, and Scott had a keen sense of justice and supported racial equality. After arriving to play at a Texan hall where the audience was segregated, she left town, arguing, "Why would people come to see a black woman play and then not want to sit next to someone just like me?" She refused to take "black woman's" roles in films and caused a three-day strike with one film company when she insisted the black members of the cast get better costumes. Scott also won a lawsuit against a restaurant where staff had refused to serve Scott and her friend because of their color. So, obviously, a troublemaker.

However, Scott won her case and the rights of African-Americans to challenge discrimination, inspiring civil rights organizations to pressure for equality in public places. She asked the committee to ensure accusations were not brought against innocent artists without proof. She won her case, but her career nose-dived, as did her marriage. Her show was canceled, and she left America for Paris, where her apartment became a mecca for American exiles and visitors, including Lester Young, Mary Lou Williams, Dizzy Gillespie, Max Roach, and musicians from the Ellington and Basie bands. She returned briefly to America to record with Charles Mingus and Max Roach (*Relaxed Piano Moods* (Debut 1955)), now regarded as one of jazz's most important recordings and inducted into National Public Radio's Basic Jazz Record Library. Inadvertently, America's discrimination succeeded in creating a center of musicians in Paris. Scott died in 1981, leaving a legacy of important changes in music and many people's lives. Even though it was canceled, her TV show provided a beacon of hope for African-American female entertainers.

There were other influencers, and game changers, without whose influence some of the most excellent musicians we have in jazz may not have achieved the heights they did. The people whose names are recalled easily are legendary for a reason, but behind their success are people who championed their cause.

## JOHN HAMMOND

ONE SUCH MAN was John Hammond. Born in 1910, he was a wealthy, middle-class New Yorker. At the time, segregation was normal, and New York had neighborhoods where different colored people rarely met or mixed. Real jazz music was played mainly by black musicians, but the Hammond neighborhood preferred swing or more sedate jazz.

John Hammond would listen to jazz music coming up from below stairs in his parents' home. He was learning piano and violin and had a musical ear. When he was thirteen, he visited London and heard a band called The Georgians, playing Dixieland jazz. Then he saw a show called *Dixie to Broadway*, featuring clarinetist Sidney Bechet, and was hooked.

When he got home, Hammond began visiting Harlem to seek out jazz recordings, something he continued throughout his school years. He had to travel because, at the time, record labels marketed different jazz music to different areas. For example, those sold to Harlem residents were on "race labels" aimed at African-Americans, and included Vocalion, Victor, and Okeh. Hammond studied violin at Yale, but his first job was working for the *Portland Evening News* under Ernest Gruening. In 1930 he became the US correspondent for the UK-based magazine *Melody Maker*. In 1931, Hammond funded the recording of pianist Garland Wilson and moved to Greenwich Village, where he set up a regular live jazz program and wrote about social divisions. In 1932 he paid for time slots on the WEVD radio station and chose musicians as guests regardless of age, race, or anything else. His guests included Art Tatum and Benny Carter. He did this until the station moved its headquarters to the Broadway Central Hotel, where black musicians were required to use the service entrance. Hammond left. He supported civil rights and wrote in his memoirs, "I heard no color line in the music."

Hammond's work for *Melody Maker* proved crucial as it linked the UK and US markets. He arranged for Columbia in America to provide recordings to its UK branch, allowing easier access to American music. He recorded saxophonist Benny Carter, violinist Joe Venuti, and pianist and bandleader Fletcher Henderson. His knowledge of the jazz of Harlem and his friendship with many musicians meant they trusted him. With his support, Benny Goodman hired black musicians like Charlie Christian and percussionist Lionel Hampton, and he was crucial in the careers of Count Basie and many others. He brought the Count Basie Orchestra from Kansas to New York for Billie Holiday's recording debut and oversaw the orchestra play two concerts at Carnegie Hall. These featured Sidney Bechet, singer Ida Cox, blues harmonica player Sonny Terry, and others.

As a reporter, Hammond was not afraid to raise questions, such as whether singer Bessie Smith would have survived the car crash she was involved in had she received treatment at the first hospital she was taken to. A car driven by a white man with his wife as a passenger hit Smith's car. The ambulances took the couple and Smith to a hospital where the couple received treatment, but Smith's ambulance was sent to another hospital as the first one was whites only. Smith died, and it is not known if prompter treatment would have saved her. Hammond reported the incident, which raised questions of whether discrimination may have played a part in her death.

After military service in World War Two, Hammond rejoined Columbia but disliked the bebop scene that had arisen and left jazz, concentrating on other genres. He signed singer Pete Seeger, percussionist and social reform activist Babatunde Olatunji, Aretha Franklin, and Bob Dylan but never lost his respect for jazz. People like him, resolute in the purpose of bringing good jazz to everyone regardless of color or race, and being well placed to do so, made a real impact.

## JAZZ INFLUENCERS IN OTHER GENRES

JAZZ MUSICIANS HAVE always had connections to other musical genres. Artists including Miles Davis, Herbie Hancock, and Robert Glasper have fused jazz with different music. Davis was accused of "selling out" when he played at events such as the Isle of Wight Festival in 1970 when he took his *Bitches Brew* band and performed jazz-rock to the largest audience a jazz musician had ever played. With the changing scene in America, jazz clubs closing and reopening as rock or disco venues, Davis knew he had to "reinvent" jazz as music for the masses. So, he took his band—saxophonist Gary Bartz, pianist Keith Jarrett, keyboardist Chick Corea, bassist Dave Holland, drummer Jack DeJohnette, and percussionist Airto Moriera and played alongside rock artists including Jimi Hendrix, The Who, The Doors, and Chicago. Davis performed an extensive set and introduced an audience of an estimated 600,000 to jazz at its best. This was not the jazz people expected but high-energy music with contrasting driving grooves and contemplative interludes. The crowd was enthralled, and Davis, in his sparkly suit and lacquered horn, introduced a new generation to jazz rhythms and patterns. Wayne Shorter and musicians Davis had played with earlier in his career had formed their own bands, performing different kinds of jazz. However, Davis set about revitalizing the jazz industry. Jazz could no longer be called "aloof" or "elite."

Another musician who had played with Davis was Herbie Hancock. After parting ways with Davis, he released rock, funk, electronic sounds, and jazz albums. His 1983 release "Rockit" (Columbia 1983) merged jazz, electronic music, and hip hop. This record influenced artists across the globe, selling millions. Hancock had previously released *Monster* (Columbia 1980), which was rock-based with jazz elements, and *Quartet* (CBS/Sony 1982)—a straight-ahead jazz album with Wynton Marsalis, Ron Carter, and Tony Williams. Hancock's recordings nearly all used jazz-influenced phrases and rhythms. Seemingly uninterested in conforming to a label, Hancock took influences from what he heard around him. Every time Hancock produced new music, it departed radically from his previous recordings, presenting what must have seemed a marketing nightmare for his label. However, he proved an astute and highly commercial musician. Hancock remains a jazz, rock/pop/R&B, funk legend, proving, if any proof were needed, genre-linking possibilities and how deeply ensconced jazz is in the mix.

Other important people changed the way jazz music was perceived. These include Francis Wolff, whose photographs were integral to the rise of the Blue Note record label, and Manfred Eicher, founder of ECM. This label supported both mainstream and experimental jazz musicians.

I think everyone has a different set of people who, to their way of thinking, changed everything. For some, it might be a particular teacher or record label manager. For others, it was an encouraging relative, but most musicians point to other musicians. I asked them to share these.

Musician and producer Dan O'Callaghan said, "I would say Bird (Charlie Parker). Pre-bebop is different music to my ears."

Composer and conductor Sam Eastmond agreed with Parker as a choice. He said, "You need Charlie Parker in that list and Miles Davis. Every revolution is preceded by the previous one. Monk, Mingus, and Ellington also left deep and indelible marks. Ellington, Gil Evans, Carla Bley, Don Ellis, Bob Brookmeyer on the large ensemble side. All essential and lead to Maria Schneider and Darcy James. Also Coltrane! The big, obvious ones are the big, obvious ones for a reason. People know about them because they reshaped the direction. Nothing post 'Trane is unaffected, and there are so many marginal figures who change so much who get ignored, which gets personal; Eldridge, Edison, Young, seem huge to me, but is their impact still felt, or does it manifest in the impact they had in others? Also, Lester Bowie, who made a huge amount of pop and other fusion. Butch Morris with his conduction. Wadada Leo Smith, Anthony Braxton, all more recent with huge impact. Of course, I think we tend to see innovators in harmonic/melodic terms, but also Philly Joe Jones, Elvin Jones, Jack DeJohnette, and Milford Graves cannot be overlooked."

Researcher, educator, and musician Casper Hoedemaekers added, "Louis (Armstrong), Bird, definitely. I think that the rhythmic displacement, open approach to improvisation, and angularity of phrasing of Tristano had a major impact on contemporary jazz. Monk was also a major influence on modern jazz composition."

Photographer and writer Patrick Hadfield said, "I'd include Miles Davis in the list—a key component of several movements (cool, modal, electric). And John Coltrane, for taking music way out, and then way out some more. And I agree with others—Armstrong, Ellington, Monk. And Mingus!"

Pianist and vocalist Champian Fulton agreed with Bird and added, "I would also add Basie. That rhythm section changed the idea of rhythm. Bennie Moten (bassist) and Count Basie!"

Russ Wimbish said, "I'd put Count Basie. His band redefined the swing feel to the point where we take it for granted. He added a lightness and a bounce to jazz's rhythmic drive that was absent before 1936."

Some musicians pioneered a different way of playing an instrument. For example, as bandleader, saxophonist, and entertainer Ray Gelato pointed out, "Tenor saxophonist Illinois Jacquet was a game changer. His solo on 'Flying Home' created a whole new school of R&B tenor players. Jacquet influenced Coltrane. Lester Young and Coleman Hawkins probably influenced every tenor saxophonist that came after." Illinois was just nineteen when he recorded his epic solo on Benny Goodman/Lionel Hampton's "Flying Home" in 1942. It had been recorded before in 1939 with solos from guitarist Charlie Christian, but after Jacquet's honking tenor solo with Hampton, it became a regular show closer.

I would add saxophonist Ivo Perelman, who I have written with several times. He uses the altissimo range on his tenor sax, adding an additional octave and giving the instrument a voice-like quality. Composer Sam Eastmond cites Bill Frisell, saying, "He incorporates huge amounts of 'non-jazz' language. It is hard to find a guitarist not moved by him. He's pretty seminal, and it is worth looking at the sheer amount of situations he's played in. His *Quiver* album with Ron Miles and Brian Blade might be a good entry point. Also, with Hemphill and Zorn. Plus, everything he's done under his own name."

Patrick Hadfield added some more, and said, "Most bass players pinpoint James (Jimmy) Blanton, who played in a very pizzicato manner, Scott LaFaro, and drummers Max Roach and Elvin Jones."

Drummer Will Glaser gave his list of game changers as Baby Dodds, Zutty Singleton, Chick Webb, Papa Jo Jones, Kenny Clarke, Max Roach, Roy Haynes, Philly Joe Jones, Elvin Jones, Ed Blackwell, Sunny Murray, Paul Motian, and Jon Christensen. "But," he added, "it's so hard to boil it down."

For composer Rick Simpson, innovators were Art Tatum, Duke Ellington, and Nat King Cole. Saxophonist Susanne Alt said, "Tony Williams, Art Blakey, Jeff Tain Watts, Bill Stewart, and Chris Dave." Sam Eastmond added more—Jack DeJohnette and Milford Graves.

Jazz appreciator (and virologist) Nigel Wallis gave his game changers as Cecil Taylor, Evan Parker, Peter Brötzmann, Manfred Eicher, Jost Gebers, George Wein (founder of the Newport Jazz Festival and one of the founders of the New Orleans Jazz and Heritage Festival).

Bass clarinet player Jason Stein's list includes John Zorn, Wynton Marsalis, Evan Parker, and Cecil Taylor. American producer and keyboard player Jason Miles included Miles Davis, Pat Metheny, Bill Evans, and Jaco Pastorius.

Detroit-based journalist, critic, and author of *Jazz from Detroit* (University of Michigan Press, 2019) Mark Stryker put his finger on the difficulty when he said, "The challenge is to get at the essence of jazz history in the fewest names possible. Miles Davis once said you could sum up jazz history in four words: Louis Armstrong, Charlie Parker. I think it takes eight: Louis Armstrong, Duke Ellington, Charlie Parker, Ornette Coleman. However, I hasten to add that Ornette was still deeply connected to the tradition. Principally he was still a blues musician, and swinging remained central to his vocabulary. It's about improvisers who fundamentally opened new wings of the art form. More than anyone, Ornette liberated the music from standard harmony, rhythm, and form. He remains ground zero for everything related to free jazz. 'Trane opened a new wing too in many ways. He embodied the shift from bebop (Bird) into post-bop modality/harmony. But you can still argue that many of 'Trane's innovations were related to bebop in key ways, whereas Ornette was a more radical break with the past."

Teacher and composer Anthony Cornicello said, "When I've taught jazz history, I say that the first portion of the class is about Louis (Armstrong), and the latter part is about Miles (Davis). So many connections can be made with these figures alone. Of course, Duke (Ellington) is in there also."

As Hadfield rightly says, though, "The more one considers the question, the longer the list gets."

Musicians believe most changes are like ripples in a pond, gradually moving out to a wider circle—one musician influences another, who influence more, and so on. At the same time, just occasionally, someone comes along and blows everything we thought we knew out of the water. It is interesting how the same names came up time and again. Miles Davis, John Coltrane, Duke

Ellington, Ornette Coleman, John Zorn, Herbie Hancock, Elvin Jones, Art Tatum, Thelonious Monk. Others mentioned less often but who musicians feel were influential in changing how they—and audiences—see jazz music include saxophonists Dave Koz and David Sanborn, singer Billie Holiday, trumpeter Dizzy Gillespie, pianist, bandleader, and composer Chick Corea, trumpeter Chet Baker, singer Sammy Davis Junior, reedman Eric Dolphy, pianist Cecil Taylor, singer Ella Fitzgerald, pianist and composer Scott Joplin, bass guitarist Jaco Pastorius, drummer Billy Cobham, singer and guitarist George Benson, bassist Marcus Miller, pianist and singer Nina Simone, organist Jimmy Smith, pianist and composers Bud Powell and Thelonious Monk, guitarist Pat Metheny, composer and arranger Dave Grusin, and funk/soul/jazz saxophonist Grover Washington Junior.

A true game changer is a rare thing, but when they come along, they need a chance to express themselves in their music, and those enabling this need to be prepared to take a risk. So there are people behind the scenes—managers, curators, band members, and others—who make things happen but remain in the background. We also need to remember that audiences change and evolve, so what was once not accepted may be at a different time, but you don't know unless you try.

Sam Eastmond summed things up: "It is creators' jobs to be ahead of the audience. Otherwise, you get the banality of 'give the people what they want.' Great for entertainment, terrible for art. Artists should push audiences. The closer you get to the present, the more marginal the music becomes, so the most radical innovators often have less impact globally or their effect is more contained. Which doesn't diminish their importance."

The great thing is when you get into jazz and find your particular game changers, people who, for you, mean nothing after them was the same, you will argue with the choices here and give many reasons why your preferences should be on the lists. And that is a good thing—we all have our favorites.

# CHAPTER 4

## *Society and jazz*

SINCE JAZZ BEGAN, there has been little physical distance between those performing and those watching. Marching bands and street performers play in
front of their observers, and many jazz gigs are in venues with little separation
between the musicians and audience. So, it is natural that the music reflects
reactions to current and immediate situations. It is not as easy for an orchestra playing Mozart to react to a natural disaster as a jazz ensemble with
five members free to express themselves in the music. Improvisation allows
musicians to change how they play with each performance. I have seen a jazz
group performing shortly after the sudden death of their beloved pianist. It
was extraordinary how different members took what would have been the
piano lines and demonstrated their sense of loss and respect. Improvisation
allows this expression.

### LOOKING INTO THE SOUND MIRROR

WE WOULD ALL like to believe we would never be party to racism, discrim-
INATION, OR INJUSTICE. Yet we know deep down our society has, and jazz music
has always reflected how we are as people. Jazz also celebrates and toasts the
good in people and happy events.

At the turn of the twentieth century in America, segregation and discrimination were just how things were, and there were different expectations for
different parts of society. Women were meant to be supportive rather than
leaders; different races were considered superior to others, and, in the words of
Miles Davis's opening track on 1959's *Kind of Blue* (Columbia) album, "So What?"

Now we question such attitudes. How could incredibly talented people be
treated poorly? Or, like happened with the International Sweethearts of Rhythm
Band, how could it be right that white girls playing with black girls met with

disapproval and threats? The 'International' part of the Sweethearts' name was added to negate some of the issues which arose, especially in the Southern States when they came across people who wanted African-Americans and whites separated, even in music, and those who were wary of supporting them in case they were on the receiving end of a social backlash. When jazz became popular, America was still relatively young. There were immigrants from many parts of the world, some economic migrants, some escaping oppression and discrimination in their countries, and some wanting the American way of life. America was welcoming, and opportunities were seemingly endless. However, in reality, discrimination happened. Jewish musicians like George Gershwin, Al Jolson, Artie Shaw, and Irvin Berlin (Jacob Gershwine, Asa Yoelson, Arthur Jacob Arshawsky, and Israel Beilin, respectively) changed their performing names to "American" sounding ones to get work, and Native Americans, and many other groups, were discriminated against.

As is often the case, people began to assert their objections through music and the arts, reflecting the movements that were springing up. Civil rights and women's rights groups had set up across America and, while the rights of women made progress during the 1920s and '30s, the issues concerning civil rights remained unresolved.

During the early 1960s, civil rights movements galvanized righteous support. Malcolm X appealed to those who wanted a separation of black and white, keeping both sides pure and blacks supporting each other economically and culturally. Martin Luther King Jr. sought a peaceful solution through non-violent protest, using his evocative speeches to encourage integration and equality (a view Malcolm X came around to during the last year of his life after he visited Africa and found white people completely non-threatening). America was on the cusp of profound changes both in the laws but also, more importantly perhaps, in the mindset of its population.

Bassist John Edwards once told me he believed that when society is stagnant or self-satisfied, jazz often kick-starts movement by becoming more interesting and experimental. When society is full of unrest, jazz also responds, taking that energy, using it creatively, and transposing it into the music. Either way, jazz is a sound mirror, reflecting who we are and what we have become. It has been this way for decades, and musicians are often the first to challenge accepted canons and highlight societal wrongs.

As early as 1935, jazz musicians used their celebrity to change perceptions. Benny Goodman, himself the son of Russian immigrants, brought the supremely talented pianist Teddy Wilson into his orchestra, followed by vibraphonist Lionel Hampton and drummer Gene Krupa. Goodman also used arrangements by bandleader Fletcher Henderson for his radio shows—demonstrating the quality lies in musical talent, nothing else. He did this while, in some states, integration in orchestras was still not happening.

Jazz is full of creative people, and if society is not right, they will instigate change.

# JAZZ SOCIETY TODAY

JAZZ TODAY REFLECTS more sectors of society than ever. Not long back, a venue manager told me he thought one of the reasons jazz had not become mainstream was that people liked being part of a niche group in the past. That also explains why jazz got sidelined by even the media—many people couldn't break into the groups or understand the ridiculous terms: noodling, woodshedding, chops, changes. He made me smile as he did the "jazzers' face"—eyes closed, mouth turned down, head bobbing, shut off, and unreachable. He described how some of the people who came to clubs in the 1960s and '70s dressed—little beards, bright shirts, fitted jackets, pointy shoes (for some reason), or a beret and big glasses. (A bit like hipsters today, except hipsters are friendly and have man buns).

Now things are different. In a jazz venue, nothing feels elite or niche. No longer solely the domain of men, jazz clubs are filled with life, laughter, and, of course, music. Your culture or background is not as important as what you bring. Soak in the atmosphere, the camaraderie, sharing, and passion for jazz. Women are more welcome. One jazz musician said recently as we sat in a club, "Sheesh! It used to be everyone in this club, week in, week out, was a man. Now, the doorman is a woman, the barman is a woman, heck even the toilet is unisex, and look at the band—TWO female musicians!" He then grinned at me, winked, and added, "I love it. Everyone is here—including my daughter!"

The social demographic has changed dramatically in the last decade. The mix is more even, primarily due to efforts by festival managers, venue owners, and the change in society's attitudes.

There is another reason, a trick some venues nearly missed. Women have power. They earn more than in the past, they are media savvy, and jazz venues want some of that income coming their way. They also want the kudos of promoting male and female artists equally. Jazz is not there yet in terms of gender equality, but progress is being made—more on this later.

With an increase in females in all areas, and media initiatives supporting female writers, photographers, and critics who promote women in jazz, the scene is changing to reflect society's changing values and emphasis. Young people see jazz as the real alternative music, and seeing more young people on stage encourages them to attend jazz concerts and festivals.

## MONEY IN POCKETS

JAZZ HAS ENRICHED our existence beyond measure, yet it seems we give little back in terms of financial support for those creating it. Given the low returns for streaming, the increasing expectations of audiences to access free music, and the high level of competition, I wondered how musicians make a living. Do gigs pay well? I have seen musicians selling CDs and other merchandise after gigs. Does this generate much income? So often, musicians tell me they get thousands upon thousands of streams for their music and yet make a miniscule amount of money, so how do they make a living? A guitar player I know recently told me that after a gig an audience member came up and told him, "That was great. I bought your CD and copied it for three of my friends. They like it too." I asked how he reacted (to the loss of three sales), and he said, "Well, I just sort of went, 'thank you, glad you enjoyed it.' I was so taken aback." A few people said they might have said something a little harsher in his shoes, but it is not easy when it is just you and your audience.

Things seemed more straightforward when a musician recorded for a label; they sold the albums and paid them royalties. You either made it, or you failed. Now, things are different because more people make records, but the money generated by sales is small, so it begs the question: how much do musicians make from gigging, and how much do they earn from related (or unrelated) work?

Bandleader Ray Gelato told me, "I managed to make a living for thirty-five years leading my band, but also key was being open to guest spots and other collaborations, in other words, diversifying. We also kept active with our merchandise. I can't say the same now as it's gotten much harder."

Composer and label owner Ian Boddy explained further, "It's good to have several musical income streams. Mine come from library music royalties, sound design and running the DiN label, as well as releasing my own music."

Professor Stephen Palmer said, "Some composers/producers sell their tracks under a license for various uses, for example, background, film, TV, events, adverts, and online radio. They charge a one-off fee upfront. I've purchased great tracks from the filmmusic.io site, and there's no additional charge if you aren't a pro member."

Philip Booth added, "Many of the busiest musicians have day jobs—some in music education, or in a job tangentially related to music, or some (like me) in a completely different profession. Gigs don't pay the bills."

Saxophonist Phil Meadows said, "I tend to see musicians and artists as having different, yet interchangeable roles. I feel like a musician when my role has a purpose predominantly for others but an artist when I am employed for my self-expression. In my experience, I feel more of a musician when I'm playing a theater show or corporate function and more of an artist when I'm producing, orchestrating/conducting a project, or performing original music—either my own or with the composer. At times, being an artist has been my major employer, but being a musician has always been something I can rely on. For me, there's a real thrill to being the artist because you're employed because you are you and not because you are one of several, but both roles are brilliant!"

Joe Higham said he had observed that since the late 1980s, many conservatoires and academies have been more open and provided musicians with teaching work. Higham teaches music in secondary school and plays professionally.

Composer Andy Quin advised, "One trick is to get your stuff available for licensing to be used for productions/ads/games, etc. You then earn royalties from performances and broadcasts. If you are lucky, you can earn millions this way while doing something you love."

Saxophonist and radio host Guido Spannocchi said his income was, "A mix and match of functions, funding, sales of albums and tours. In my case, digital income is negligible," while bassist Ivan Tenorio says, "In my case: gigs eighty percent, from corporate to social to jazz club; teaching fifteen percent and the rest is recording or busking. Some film scoring now and then, but those gigs are hard to get."

Composer and pianist Roland Perrin said, "Teaching is about seventy-five to eighty percent of my income. Gigs and commissions account for the rest."

Singer and comedian Phat King Cole, based in Paris, said, "I busk in the subway as part of a community project sponsored by the city's transport system (transit). I have used that as a platform to engage with commuters who have become supporters who helped me when I needed it most, for example, during the recent lockdown. There are similar projects in London, NYC, and Toronto."

Singer Marvin Muoneke says, "All of the income-generating methods mentioned here are great and valid, especially busking. I think the key to making as much of a living as possible as a professional musician is to have your fingers dipped in numerous pies. What I mean by that is to expand and diversify your business by doing solo, duo, trio, quartets, etc. If you can get involved with bands who are gigging regularly, corporate gigs, and a few residencies, then I believe it's achievable to make your main income derive from music."

Trumpeter Freddie Gavita and trombonist Gareth Roberts told me that most musicians teach and play, and engagements can include corporate functions and gigs. Teaching work includes schools, colleges, and private lessons.

The founder of Hot Club Philadelphia, guitarist and teacher Barry Wahrhaftig, explained how it is possible to earn from several areas using a broad range of interfaces. He explained, "We have always sold CDs at gigs. Our music is on iTunes, Bandcamp, etc., and can be streamed, but the physical CDs and downloads are best. Streaming pays crap. I think it is a fraction of a cent per stream. If you sell CDs, you may as well license for streaming. Not everyone has a CD player, so I have used download cards, which are inexpensive cost-wise to the artists and can be sold for less than a CD. Things are changing so much all of the time. I used not to opt-in for Spotify-type services; bigger venues want to see your follower stats. I am considering vinyl, but it's higher in cost and takes a few months to produce."

In all cases, the sale of merchandise provides additional income. I ran a one-day festival in London and one of the most important questions for the musicians was whether or not there would be a merchandise stall where they could sell CDs, mugs, tee shirts and other goods to fans. These "add-on" sales are vital for musicians' incomes.

Streaming is an accessible, easy way to listen to music. Different platforms offer services of varying quality and price. When you stream music, you may wonder how much of your money goes to the artist. What do you think? Fifty percent? Thirty percent? Ten percent even? The truth is virtually nothing goes to the artist. They get around $0.003 to $0.004 per stream, which, when you consider they create the content which the sites sell to their listeners, is pretty rubbish rates.

To put this into context, a million streams will generate around $3-4000 for an artist. And a million streams is a lot.

When you consider the studio hire, the costs of hiring each musician, power, transport, production, materials, and distribution costs, streaming is no way to earn a living.

Using just a couple of examples, one composer whose music is used for films, video games, adverts, and a host of other media shared with me that one (very short) track of his music was downloaded 7.63 million times and he got—wait for it—656.74. He only got a tiny amount for each download as the track was very short, but even so, $656.74 is very little return for nearly 77 million downloads. Luckily, this musician has downloads in the billions due to the diverse nature of his output and the use of his compositions for games, videos, etc., so he told me it does add up—eventually. But how many musicians get this number of downloads or have such a diverse output?

Another musician had placed his self-released music on several platforms and gave me the figures from each after 100 downloads. Amazon paid 40 pence, Deezer 40 pence, Tidal £1.00, Apple 40 pence, and Spotify 30 pence.

So, when you see social media posts like, "I just topped 3,500 downloads for the record. Maybe that chocolate bar in celebration is a step closer," it is only partially in jest.

Popular with musicians are the marketplace sites, with Bandcamp being the most popular, but even as I write, major changes are happening with some of these sites, and their community-building areas are seeing profound changes.

It seems that most jazz musicians make their living by a mix of performing, teaching, and selling music or their skills in other ways—quite an eye-opener. Of course, wealthy artists have people to perform most roles, but for most musicians, even successful ones, such as those I spoke to, being a jazz musician is a tough choice for a career, and you need to be skilled in many areas.

# THE C-WORD

COVID-19 AND THE lockdowns that went with it had a lasting effect on musicians. Their incomes vanished overnight with the cancellation of concerts, and studios were suddenly forbidden areas. Their income instantly fell off a cliff for many—not just musicians but venues, managers, PR agencies, caterers, technicians, and more. It was unexpected, unseen, and felt like an ambush. Where there had been a steady stream of gigs, festivals, tours, and recording events, the diary pages turned blank. How did musicians and venues plan? How did they stay in touch with the people who would be their lifelines in the future?

As well as income, jazz provides a purpose, fulfills creative needs, and unites people. Like those from other genres, jazz musicians had to develop inventive ideas and new actions and instigate ways of doing things to enable them to survive financially and stay connected creatively. Venues, too, had to reimagine business models to stay afloat and keep people engaged if they were to stand any chance of reopening once the lockdowns were over.

A few venues were awarded grants from the government and funding bodies. Some musicians found ways of tapping into government financial help, but this did not resolve their need to make music, progress in their art, and connect with people. The uncertain length of time the lockdowns would last and how long distancing measures would be in place made the future an unknown landscape. What would that landscape even look like? Would things ever be the same even if they got through lockdowns?

Musicians approached the situation with admirable determination. Jazz went online, people released amazing music and found ways to come together, record, create concerts, and turn something potentially negative into something that continued to give pleasure, connect audiences and generate at least some income. They worked with technology, and I was party to many conversations where people were swapping technical know-how. It also led to an appreciation of the technical guys.

That annoying few seconds delay on the early online meetings was resolved, meaning people could play live together and not have to allow for the gap and edit performances afterward. It was truly amazing to see how creative people could be, and musicians thought about how they might use this opportunity. Collaborations happened between artists who would never have met under normal circumstances. Online performances allowed people to see bands who would usually play far from their location. The number and quality of people playing online increased hugely. Performances could either be paid for with a "ticket" being an invitation to the meeting, or they had a "donate" button that viewers could use to donate to the artist as they played.

Online concerts also enabled so that those for whom getting to a concert was usually complex—disabled, elderly, or housebound with children and so on—could access gigs and see their favorite performers. Venues found ways to support both artists and themselves by holding online auctions selling recordings, and once small groups were allowed to gather, they hosted live-streamed gigs. Some of these events got more paying online attendees than the venue would typically hold.

For some, the confusing messages from governments about whether they could play or not and the dramatic fall of income and insecurity about the future meant they left the music industry, but many musicians stayed, and some even gained new fans due to their online content and presence.

Musicians also kept connected to their fans and each other by hosting coffee mornings, chats, and even virtual festivals.

I interviewed many musicians during the pandemic, and something that came up many times was how they missed playing with others. For a musician, the connection and feedback from fellow players is paramount—some even said they did not realize just how much they got from this until it was taken away. All bar one missed their audiences too, and while the travel respite was welcome for a short time, many ached to get back on the road and play to fans in different countries again.

The Covid pandemic also took some of the beloved jazz musicians who were still performing and sharing their music with the world—including pianist Ellis Marsalis Jr., trumpeter Wallace Roney, and others.

Now in post-pandemic times, live music is returning with a vengeance. Nearly every day, I hear from a musician going on tour or playing a major venue—and many playing small ones too. The venues are encouraging, and the audiences are hungry to see as much live music as possible. I am seeing the results of online connections made during the pandemic as musicians who would never have met are now inviting people to their locality for residencies or to start a tour. Ronnie Scott's, Cafe OTO, and many other clubs have reopened to packed houses. It is genuinely incredible how live music has come back.

It is as if the music feels even more precious now we have had an enforced break. Since the world opened up again, I have seen many acts and enjoyed every one of them, felt safe, and I appreciate live music again—and those performing. You can read more about the innovative ways musicians worked in the articles and books listed at the end of this book.

Even with the innovations and support, the impact of the Covid-19 lockdowns on musicians' incomes was severe. According to a BBC report, in the UK, a third of musicians and those in related employment (venue staff, studio managers, etc.) lost their jobs during the lockdowns. The music industry lost close to US$10 billion in sponsorship in the US. The richness of jazz—from composers, promoters, youth orchestras and education, musicians, managers, tour curators, bar staff, and more was in danger of being lost forever. According to *This Is Music 2021*, live music income fell ninety percent, and many musicians found themselves ineligible for grants or government support. The UK workforce in music-related employment fell from 197,000 to 128,000 in spite of the growth in the industry over the decade preceding Covid. I was so struck by how musicians coped and how little was written about this that I wrote *Pause, Play, Repeat*—a book featuring eighteen of them from different parts of the world (see the end of this book). Their individual stories are emotive and impressive, as they strove to maintain their presence.

The pandemic also led to people accessing music differently. Physical sales showed a fall, which was expected given the situation, but so did digital sales. Streaming saw a massive increase, and people chose to watch and hear music on TVs, computers, and other screens.

Though we are emerging from the impact of the Covid-19 pandemic, it has already changed many things, including music and how we listen to it. Many musicians realized the value of online gigs and allowed access to more people, so some will continue live work alongside online performances.

More people listen to music now on handheld devices and home TVs. Some streaming platforms saw considerable increases in subscriber numbers and increased on-demand video streams. People listened to music at different times because of the removal of the commute, and they listened to more music during the week, whereas previously, listening rose at the weekend. A survey by the Interactive Advertising Bureau showed a significant drop in advertising on music channels.

Some artists delayed releasing music during the pandemic, but many chose to release more because people had more time to listen. Live revenue, as expected, was nearly zero.

Some funding provisions by Universal Music, some of the streaming giants, YouTube Music, and others provided support in funding being made available for artists hit by the pandemic. Some companies offered artists interest-free advances on projected royalty payments, and millions of dollars were poured into the music industry to help it survive. Performers could also borrow live streaming equipment to enable them to perform from home and be beamed into their listeners' homes.

Barry Wahrhaftig gave me a rundown of how he made it through the pandemic. "I played and hosted some stream-only shows at the beginning of the pandemic. After a few months, the donations dropped quite a bit. I ended up hosting an outdoor series last summer, and that did well. I felt I needed to be proactive, help others, and help myself in the process. We donated some of the proceeds to local charities. I did go on unemployment last year for the first time in my life. I am off it now, and there are lots of gigs for myself and the band at the moment since a lot of folks are vaxxed."

In times like lockdowns, jazz musicians prove some of the most creative individuals on the planet. Jazz has seen many changes in its history. It reflects the waves of change as the human race spirals continually. Historically, and with the gift of hindsight, the circular patterns of society can be observed. Racism was at its height when jazz began. Audiences were segregated in many places; black musicians were mistreated. Then the civil rights movement in the 1960s saw jazz react, and the music became energized, even angry and rebellious. Today, we have witnessed riots over the death of George Floyd in America, and protests about civil rights issues are happening. Jazz is again exciting, angry, and reactive. In the 1960s, there was a reaction to MLK Jr.'s death and riots over Vietnam. Today we have the anger of climate issues, and the Black Lives Matter movement has gained respect. Once, women fought for the right to vote and their place in the arts, including jazz—now we have protests over women's safety, with the death of innocent women at the hands of sexual deviants and the increase in drink spiking. We take a step forward and one back. Obama, Trump, females with power, men back in charge, the cycles of change in tiny steps and people's reactions to them goes on, and jazz, with its close and personal nature, reflects what we do right back.

✳✳✳

DURING THE 1960S, young people found rock and roll. Commercially, rock and roll had appeal, and some jazz venues even closed and reopened as rock or, later, disco haunts. Jazz could not compete with this new music, its danceable rhythms, and the fashion around it.

Rather than compete, jazz held its own. It was still played, the players continued to tour, but it felt increasingly remote and elite. TV and radio programming rarely featured jazz anymore, and people almost forgot about it. It was old-fashioned music; over.

When some of the great players, including John Coltrane, Eric Dolphy, Monk,

Armstrong, and Ellington, died, they left vacuums practically impossible to fill. There was little incentive to play jazz because, commercially, it had shrunk. Music schools outside America still frowned on jazz. Young people no longer saw other young people play jazz. The once young guns of jazz were now middle-aged elder statesmen.

Instead, young people played rock and roll, punk, metal, and disco. Jazz features in general newspapers and magazines became rarer, and the popular video channels like MTV rarely, if ever, featured jazz. Even jazz magazines did little to help because they were populated with writers who wrote about the same few musicians from the same labels and became increasingly polarized. They alienated themselves from readers due to their elitism and snobbishness. There was a sense of jazz being unconnected to other music, and the only jazz people heard outside the major clubs was in lifts, department stores, or closing out a TV show. It was sanitized, frothy; musicians like Davis and Gillespie found their circuit smaller and their careers languishing.

However, jazz was not about to relinquish its powerful voice to any other genre. Toward the end of the 1960s, the jazz renaissance began. Miles Davis, Dizzy Gillespie, Wayne Shorter, and Ron Carter slowly but surely breathed fresh life into jazz, creating change and encouraging new players, and the scene at club level expanded. People got fed up with being told what to listen to and buy. Rock, pop, and disco were commercial, mass-produced, and not very musical compared to jazz. The young of the 1970s began to seek something different—and they turned back to jazz.

But jazz had changed. Fusion brought jazz and rock, jazz and funk, jazz and R&B. The jazz legends now played with young people. The fusion from Weather Report, Davis, Hancock, and Sun Ra led to more discoveries—Pharoah Sanders, Carla Bley, Alice Coltrane. The renewed interest in jazz snowballed.

Young people breathed life back into jazz music and more venues reopened their doors to jazz musicians and audiences. Record sales, especially for fusion artists, took off. The jazz momentum has continued, and looking back, one can even say jazz possibly benefited from the temporary hiatus of the 1960s and '70s because it reinvented itself and connected again. Yet, the original music could also still be found being played. Today, traditional players still play and thrive because as people have rediscovered jazz, they have rediscovered the great players. Jazz is a happy place.

\*\*\*

AS JAZZ MATURED and outlasted changes in tastes, it got itself a history, and its effects on society could be studied. One of the significant areas where social change can be made is in education. The inclusion of jazz in so many curriculums has led to a greater understanding of the music.

Jazz began to be taught in schools during the late 1930s. One example is Piney Woods Country Life School in Jackson, Mississippi, where, from 1938, Laurence C. Jones was principal and included jazz as part of the children's musical education. He formed the Piney Woods School Band to raise funds for the school—whose pupils were mainly black children and orphans. The band went on tour, and more young women of black and mixed race were invited to join from Harlem. They would eventually become the hugely successful International Sweethearts of Rhythm.

However, despite its popularity, jazz was rarely studied until the late 1940s, when a few musicians began teaching jazz in New York, Boston, and Los Angeles. Joseph Schillinger, in Boston, began jazz teaching at Schillinger House (which became Berklee), but classical scholars viewed jazz as folk art for untrained musicians, so it took a decade or so before jazz became a valid subject.

By the 1950s, jazz could be studied at nearly forty colleges, and by the 1960s, most major colleges offered jazz options. During the 1970s until the 1990s, more colleges and universities began to include jazz studies programs. Now classical and jazz students study alongside each other and often play together. Studies can lead to a bachelor's, master's, or doctorate in jazz, and over one hundred American colleges and universities offer jazz majors. Colleges, conservatoires, and universities worldwide now offer degrees in jazz studies or jazz options. Jazz is considered a separate genre and worthy of its own pedagogy, separate skill sets, and research. Even at school level, jazz is enjoying newfound popularity as young people are exposed to more jazz through their music lessons and tutors.

Today, as those taught in the seventies and eighties become teachers and professional musicians, jazz is valued and taught well. As more knowledge is gained, the resources for students become greater. College jazz festivals and competitions provide opportunities for students to learn from experienced musicians. Issues such as diversity and equality are discussed openly, and students are aware of the need for mindful respect from early in their studies. The Jazz Education Network—an outgrowth of the International Association for Jazz Education—was set up in 2008 to encourage jazz study and build new audiences.

Doctorates in jazz can be obtained by studying at prestigious colleges, including the Eastman School of Music in Rochester, the Manhattan School of Music, New England Conservatory of Music, Leeds Conservatoire, Trinity Laban, the Guildhall School of Music & Drama, University of North Texas, and many others. Institutions like the Herbie Hancock Institute of Jazz, Berklee College, Jazz At Lincoln Center, and the Musicians Institute in Los Angeles offer many different programs, study paths, and innovative projects to get involved in. In Europe, there are many opportunities to study jazz too.

Today, jazz people like drummer and educator Terri Lyne Carrington and trumpeter, bandleader, and educator Wynton Marsalis continue to establish initiatives that create changes in education to spread their messages on equality and respect through jazz music. Carrington has helped open up opportunities for jazz education to young people from poorer areas—girls in particular. Inspired by the absence of women coming into jazz education, Carrington began the Berklee Institute of Jazz and Gender Justice, which encourages female performers.

Saxophonists Daniel Bennett and the Bosman Twins (Dwayne and Dwight) use jazz music to engage and connect with young and older students across America. Performing arts high schools including jazz in their programs have gone from just a handful in the 1970s to over one hundred today, and other countries, including Cuba, Spain, and France, have specialist colleges where jazz can be learned.

There is education of another kind, which is just as crucial for jazz musicians—the art of audience engagement. I have been in audiences where stellar musicians have come, played, gone, and left the audience bemused as there was no communication other than the music. I have also seen young players make inappropriate remarks to audience members and a young man freeze when the lights came up on an audience of just over 300 people. He was rescued by a veteran of the group who joined him and played by his side—only a few people in the audience noticed anything. One cannot teach how to craft your stage presence in theory lessons. It is a question of confidence and experience. To help with this, some venues offer college students the chance to play and get used to an audience in a public setting, and many experienced players support those new to the art of performing.

Some musicians feel the protection and support offered by undertaking jazz studies are valuable, but there comes the point when you have to go it alone. Others believe the only education needed is playing, learning, practicing, and gaining experience as a junior member of an orchestra, band, or another combo. If you feel ready, branch out as a solo artist. In the meantime, do your time, as the jazz saying goes.

# CHAPTER 5

## Cultural Jazz

JAZZ SHINES LIGHT into dark places, brings people together, and creates its own culture. I say "creates" because the cultural development of jazz is ongoing. At most jazz events, people feel they have been transported somewhere incredible, for a while at least. They have felt the crowd surge of emotion and been pleasantly ravaged by the music.

In the early days of jazz, it was played in clubs. Many jazz clubs in America were in the seedier districts of cities and became late-night haunts of musicians, alongside prostitutes and drug dealers.

Some agents and curators would exploit musicians, promising them riches that never materialized and taking advantage of their lack of commercial understanding (though many jazz musicians cottoned on to the money side of things pretty quickly). Mobsters, drug dealers, and those looking to exploit others also frequented some clubs, and jazz gained a reputation of being sleazy, subversive music.

Some of the best jazz players were reliant on drugs, which meant they attracted dealers and their entourage of suppliers and hangers-on.

Clubs were late-night dives, frequented by people still marginalized. With the record labels manipulating the music released and heard by the masses, the music played in clubs was different from that recorded on vinyl. Several jazz musicians suffered addiction, and some got themselves jail terms, including trumpeter Chet Baker, saxophonist Gerry Mulligan, vocalist and pianist Billie Holiday, and others.

The jazz scene was notoriously misogynistic, and there was overt racism. Many clubs remained segregated, and audiences in theaters were predominantly white, while players were black or of mixed race.

While a few musicians were addicted to narcotics, and some drank heavily, the majority simply wanted to play. But jazz was becoming a problem for the authorities, who viewed it as subversive. They became edgy and began to target jazz musicians—the list of those targeted by police is long, and some crimes were made up. Some jail terms were justified, but others were not. In 1955, Ella Fitzgerald and others—Gillespie, Jacquet, and promoter Norman Granz—were arrested for gambling after a concert in Houston, Texas—in fact in the break between two sets. Granz later said he believed his request that the audience be unsegregated angered the authorities. In October 1958, Thelonious Monk was detained, along with patron Baroness de Koenigswarter, by police after his car was stopped in Wilmington, Delaware. The police found narcotics in his trunk, but the search was later found to be unlawful by a judge—the police beat Monk.

## THE CABARET CARD
### —ANOTHER WAY TO BAN JAZZ MUSICIANS

JAZZ MUSICIANS HAD another type of police to watch out for—the dreaded cabaret card police. The cabaret card was a form of identification issued by the New York City Police Department from 1926–1967 and was required by any musician to work in a New York nightclub. Performers had to go to the police department every two years and be fingerprinted and photographed to renew their right to play in the city.

They could be revoked for any "infraction" deemed worthy of punishment. These might include abuse of narcotics, inappropriate dressing, obscenity, and other big and small "crimes." There were no precise rules as to what an "infraction" was. For many jazz musicians, their cabaret card was mysteriously revoked at crucial points in their career when it had maximum impact on their ability to work and support their families. In 1953, Charlie Parker lost his cabaret card for liquor infringements and wrote a letter to the authorities begging them to restore it. They eventually did, but not until the dramatic loss of income had affected Parker, his wife, and his children. Other performers who lost their cabaret cards included Thelonious Monk, who lost his card three times, Hazel Scott (who lost hers after appearing on the infamous "red list" of supposed communist sympathizers), Jackie McLean,and Billie Holiday. The loss of the cabaret card effectively barred a musician from performing in clubs because the venues would not risk falling foul of the law themselves.

Dexter Gordon, who served more than one prison sentence for drug-related crimes, left America for several years to live in Paris and then Copenhagen. When he returned to New York, his cabaret card was withheld not because of any new infraction but because of his criminal record. Some musicians, including Frank Sinatra, refused to play New York while a cabaret card was required. Others who had criminal records did not have their cards revoked.

There was inconsistency. Some musicians who lost their cards had them reinstated relatively quickly, while others didn't. The cabaret card system was yet another barrier jazz musicians had to overcome—alongside misogyny, racism, and snobbery, and some avoided playing in the city. New York was an important center for jazz, and the cabaret card system meant many important jazz musicians were regularly removed from circulation. The cards were seen by many as a way of ensuring any performer who challenged the social system as it stood would be removed from the club circuit.

New York suffered a decline in creativity, crucial for its developing music scene, so some venues began to allow musicians to play without the need for a card. Some players performed unbilled. Out-of-town venues where checks were less stringent hosted big-name jazz musicians and could offer lower fees.

New York began to be seen less as the important hub for jazz and more as a restricted and challenging city to play. Musicians sought alternative work, and some new combinations formed because different musicians from different bands lost or held their cabaret cards at different times. Some went to other cities like San Francisco because, of course, they could still get work, just not in the Big Apple.

The effect on musicians like Charlie Parker, Thelonious Monk, Dexter Gordon, Billie Holiday, and the scores of other great musicians whose cabaret cards were revoked is impossible to say. Who knows what might have happened if they had been played in more New York venues at the time? Would they have felt differently about themselves and the city had the authorities not set out seemingly to criminalize and subjugate the very act of performing jazz music? We will never know. As it was, reputations were destroyed, and minor or perceived misdemeanors could result in a musician's income vanishing. It is no wonder New York lost some of its appeal for musicians and, consequently, audiences.

An unintended side effect to all this banning and withdrawing cabaret cards was the media interest in jazz musicians, and their lives, grew. Papers love scandals and wanted to know why cards were withdrawn. Jazz became smeared with being populated by musicians with addiction and criminal lifestyles.

# ART AND JAZZ

WATCHING THE EVER-CHANGING jazz scene were others for whom the freedom in the music proved inspirational. They noted the judicial machinations, unfair rules, and laws that seemed to apply to some and not others. They loved the vibrancy and energy of the music, its layers, multicultural origins, textures, and colors. These were artists who found the players fascinating and the music a powerful stimulant. Jazz inspired them to paint, write poems and make films. The syncopated rhythms of jazz were used effectively by poets, and jazz poetry became popular. Poets including Langston Hughes, Jayne Cortez, and Amiri Baraka found a vehicle for expression. It became a powerful tool during the Harlem Renaissance movement of the 1920s (a movement primarily centered in literature, art, and music, which began in Harlem during the 1920s).

Erik Satie, whose music included many jazz references, was friends with Pablo Picasso and other cubists and wrote his ballet *Parade* in collaboration with Picasso and artist, playwright, and poet Jean Cocteau. Dutch painter Piet Mondrian's art reflected his love of Ellington and the blues. American artist Stuart Davis created energy and rhythm in his works partly inspired by his love of jazz. Jackson Pollock, Romare Bearden, and William H. Johnson were all influenced by jazz. The collaboration between artists and jazz musicians continues to this day. It is not unusual to find artists painting live portraits of musicians as they work. For example, The Vortex Jazz Club in London has a long-standing partnership with artists who produce awesome pictures of the musicians as they work.

Not only art but fashion was influenced by jazz. Hems of skirts were raised, and waists dropped to allow dancing; the cut was looser. New dances were invented—the Charleston, bunny hop, Lindy Hop, and others. Tap dancing—using hard-soled shoes to add percussive sounds—often accompanied jazz music and provided work for dancers. Women began to wear suits to clubs, and men's suits became loose-fitting trousers and colorful, well-cut jackets. With its high waist and wide lapels, the zoot suit became popular, or the contrasting "hipster" look favored by Dizzy Gillespie and Thelonious Monk, which also became trendy. Jazz had its own culture and identity.

The complex lives of some jazz musicians and their music have captured the imagination of filmmakers and authors. Films centering on specific jazz musicians' lives include *Born to Be Blue* (Chet Baker—Entertainment One 2015), *Ma Rainey's Black Bottom* (Ma Rainey—Netflix 2020), and *Miles Ahead* (Miles Davis—Sony 2016).

Jazz music creates an atmosphere so well, and many film scores have used jazz. For example, Dave Grusin's score for the 1975 film *Three Days of the Condor* (Paramount 1975) is often cited. But others include *Alexander's Ragtime Band* (20th Century Fox 1938), *Jazz on a Summer's Day* (New Yorker Films/Galaxy Attractions 1959), *The Cotton Club* (Orion 1984), *Round Midnight* (Warner 1986) and many more. *Stormy Monday* (Atlantic 1988), *Naked Lunch* (Alliance/First Independence 1991), *Whiplash* (Sony 2014), *La La Land* (Lionsgate 2016), and *Soul* (Disney/Pixar 2020).

There have been documentaries on musicians including Sonny Rollins,

Duke Ellington, Charles Mingus, Charlie Parker, Tubby Hayes, Courtney Pine, and TV and radio series documenting the rise of jazz.

Books on jazz musicians include Stuart Nicholson's *Ella Fitzgerald: A Biography of the First Lady of Jazz* (Da Capo Press 1994), Laurence Bergreen's *Louis Armstrong: An Extravagant Life* (Bantam Dell 1997), Jeroen de Valk's *Chet Baker: His Life and Music* (Uitgeverij Aspek B.V. 2017), Nigel Barnes' *Willow Weep for Me: The Life of Billie Holiday* (Independent 2019), and many more.

Charlie Parker may have performed well when he was high, but musicians today find this condition less conducive to productive playing—and their peers would frown on it. Today, jazz culture is pretty wholesome, and musicians better manage their private lives. They are far more likely to make an impact for their education and innovation than womanizing, hard-drinking, or drug-taking.

Jazz helped open people's eyes to the absurdity of discrimination. First, when the Italian and mixed-race bands on the riverboats exported jazz along the tributaries of the Mississippi, and second when large swing orchestras began to use musicians of different races, which created respect for musicians regardless of race. From the ranks of these swing bands, many well-known jazz musicians found fame, including Johnny Hodges, Charlie Christian, and Harry James.

Cultural changes came about from the club settings too. These gave women the beginnings of a sense of power because they allowed a looser dress code. Women also found opportunities to step out of the traditional supportive role and became managers, tour organizers, curators, and joined jazz ensembles—maybe even becoming soloists or leaders.

Jazz gave us unintended cultural benefits. Players in the UK took the sounds they had from America and worked them very "Britishly." People like Ronnie Scott, George Melly, Humphrey Lyttleton, Chris Barber, and others helped develop a quintessentially British jazz scene.

Europe benefited from jazz as many Americans settled there, especially in France, after World War One. They brought with them marching jazz tunes. The Nazis forced them home in the 1930s, but many returned later and brought jazz with them. France developed a thriving jazz scene. Clubs like the Tabou in Paris, were popular. French jazz festivals included stars such as Miles Davis, the Charlie Parker Quintet, and Sidney Bechet—who had achieved superstar status in Paris. Some found a far more appreciative and less racial audience than back home. Several musicians, including Dexter Gordon, Don Cherry, and others, found living in Europe more conducive to their music than remaining in America. So, inadvertently, disagreements and unstable environments at home for some US players gave Europe a jazz scene that developed along its own path. This was accentuated even more when the MU and AFM disputes occurred in the 1950s (see Chapter 3).

# FESTIVAL CULTURE

FESTIVALS ARE A big part of jazz culture today. They became established toward the end of the 1940s and grew in size and popularity during the '50s and '60s. While some concentrated only on jazz, others included many genres. In the stifling atmosphere after the Second World War, festivals provided a place where audiences and musicians could meet, mingle and both create, hear and see fantastic music. The importance of festivals is huge today.

According to a UK Music report in 2020, UK music festivals contribute almost £6 billion to the economy in 2019. Music festival attendance increased by 6% to 5.2 million in 2019 from 4.9 million in 2018.

Music tourism has been an area of consistent growth, and the level of spending at festivals and concerts was £4.7 billion in the UK in 2019, up 6% from £4.5 billion in 2018. Jazz festivals have social, political, creative, and economic benefits. According to the submission to the Digital, Culture, Media and Sport Committee inquiry into "The Future of UK Music Festivals" on behalf of the All Party Parliamentary Jazz Appreciation Group, each £1 spent at a jazz festival is estimated to generate £6 for the local economy. In 2019, overseas visitors spent an average of £899 compared to the average spend of domestic visitors of £183.

In comparison, the Cape Town Jazz Festival is estimated to contribute around 700 million rands to the South African economy (about US$41 million).

In New Orleans, the Jazz and Heritage Festival generates around US$300 million for New Orleans and the surrounding area. Musicians have told me about the importance of festivals in Copenhagen in Denmark, Jakarta in Indonesia, Berlin in Germany, Montreal in Canada, Montreux in Switzerland, and many other festivals, from Tokyo in Japan to Bogota in Columbia. I have seen firsthand how a jazz festival brings people together in Quito, Ecuador.

Jazz festivals and concerts provide cultural benefits as well as financial ones. They are sites for learning and personal development for musicians, audiences, and crew. The association with particular towns helps create an identity and generates positive value in terms of tourism. Examples of places associated strongly with jazz festivals include Cheltenham, London, and Swanage in the UK, and in America, Detroit, Boston, Kansas, and New Orleans, but there are many we could add to the lists and more in Europe (Copenhagen, Ljubljana, Rotterdam, Paris, Oslo, Helsinki,), not to mention more in Africa (Cape Town, South Africa, Saint Louis, Senegal), and Asia (New Delhi, Taipei).

Festival events affect the companies who deliver stages, lights, toilet blocks, and camping grounds; the list is extensive. Around festivals are associated businesses, including food and drinks vendors, book readings, poetry, comedy shows, book sales, art and craft stalls, local goods, and CD sales, with significant social, economic, and networking benefits. Jazz festivals provide a range of additional benefits to performers, such as playing to an audience that isn't made up of a band's existing fan base, which is helpful for development and stagecraft. They also provide a relatively safe environment to immerse yourself in local culture.

Local jazz gigs, too, benefit communities. Bars, cafés, and transport systems around a club will see increased trade, not to mention the catering provided within a club. So, the value of live performance in social and monetary terms is evident.

One of the keys to creating a more diverse audience is increasing diversity on stage. Where venues ensure their stages host performers of different cultures, ages, and genders, the audience reflects this. Festival and venue curators have told me that the broader the range of musicians, the wider the audience demographics—so, for them, this means more bums on seats and more revenue.

# DRUGS AND ALCOHOL?

THERE IS A persistent perception that jazz is populated by addicts of one sort or another (not just to the music). Much of this assumption is based on historical events, with some jazz musicians becoming addicted to drugs, serving jail sentences, and the sensations created in the media when a cabaret card was revoked. Events that make headlines do so generally because they are rare, so much of the talented playing that happened every night of the week went unreported. We should not forget that some charges were trumped up, and jazz musicians were targeted due to their color and a distrust of the jazz scene as a whole.

Undeniably some of the greatest jazz musicians took drugs. Heroin and cannabis were probably the main ones, and drink was often part of the way of life too. Lester Young died due to the effects of alcohol on his body. The effects of drugs were devastating, as they usually are, and Charlie Parker was probably the only musician who could play and compose iconic music while high. The drugs had a disastrous effect on his body, though, and when he died, the doctor called to attend thought he was far older than he was. He died tragically young, as did several iconic musicians. A few died of overdoses, but most from the long-term effects drugs had on their organs. Because they were famous and the media loved scandal, their addictions were reported with relish.

Many musicians of the past did not take drugs and drank moderately or not at all. Some, like Coltrane, kicked their drug habits, and Dizzy Gillespie reduced his alcohol intake once he realized he was drinking primarily out of boredom and it did not help his music.

I have heard many stories from musicians who toured during the 1970s who told me how they used to gather after gigs and share joints and beer, but the culture has changed.

Today, jazz people come from every part of society—the audiences are growing. Of the many thousands of people who go to gigs or play jazz, some will take drugs regularly and drink to excess, but the same is true of any large cohort of people. The idea that the scene is full of junkies and alcoholics is a myth. Jazz encourages vice no more than any other art form. If you go to a performance and someone is under the influence of narcotics, you are likely to see them ejected, because, for a business, reputation is everything.

## JAZZ IN PICTURES – PHOTOGRAPHERS

WHAT CATCHES YOUR eye? What makes you take a second look? From album covers to illustrations in sleeve notes, the way music is presented is crucial. Photographers need to understand how to capture a musician deep into their music, in the zone, or engaging with others or audience members. Often, images tell part of a story that words cannot, and a photographer's skill is capturing just that right moment. Cover shots can make a CD, vinyl, or tape stand out and convey a visual image to the purchaser, indicating perhaps the essence of the music within. Knowing the best light, the exact moment to take the shot, and how it might affect the viewer can take a lifetime to learn.

Some outstanding photographers, including David Laskowski, Monika Jakubowska, Tatiana Gorilovsky, and Rory Merry, have taken shots that are beautiful interpretations of musicians. Many photographers' work has proved important in jazz. These include Herman Leonard, who captured some great jazz musicians and produced work for album covers while working for promoter Norman Granz. His work appeared in *Downbeat* and *Metronome* magazines, and for twenty-five years he worked in Paris for Barclay records, capturing stunning images of stars, alongside working for fashion houses Yves St Laurent and Dior. His images of iconic stars, including Billie Holiday and Ella Fitzgerald, are stunning and capture them both onstage and in moments of contemplation.

Don Hunstein worked for Columbia Records in the 1950s until the 1980s and contributed pictures for album covers. He captured people perfectly, and his images include Miles Davis, Leonard Bernstein, and Carlos Santana. Probably his most memorable work was on the cover of Bob Dylan's 1963 album *The Freewheelin' Bob Dylan*.

William Claxton has produced iconic pictures of Chet Baker, Dinah Washington, and artists outside jazz, including Steve McQueen. His work appears in many books and magazines, including *Paris Match* and *Vogue*.

William Gottlieb worked from the late 1930s, when he started up a jazz column on the *Washington Post*, illustrated with his own shots, until the late 1940s, producing a body of work so rich, some of his pictures were inducted into the Library of Congress collection. His subjects include Louis Armstrong, Dizzy Gillespie, Gene Krupa, Thelonious Monk, Billie Holiday, Duke Ellington, and more jazz greats. He wrote for *Downbeat*, authoring scores of articles, including detailed ones on Ella Fitzgerald, and wrote children's stories. His 1979 book *The Golden Age of Jazz* (Quartet 1979) is one of the iconic collections of jazz photographs and was reprinted twelve times to meet demand.

Francis Wolff was a skilled photographer and an executive for Blue Note, whose cover work helped capture the imaginations of Blue Note purchasers, and his decision-making about recording artists proved integral to the label's success. He also documented the label's history by photographing every Blue Note recording session, documenting jazz's history on the label, and preserving it. He had a knack for capturing musicians off guard, at moments of thought or while laughing together, as well as in the moment of intense creativity. His images of John Coltrane, in particular, seem to capture the musician's essence, but Clifford Brown, Don Cherry and Ornette Coleman, and many others were also captured in exquisite portraits. He took over 30,000 pictures of jazz musicians, permanently capturing fleeting moments for future viewers.

Behind the scenes. Lights and rigging. Preparation is vital for any performance.

Photo credit: Luciano Rossetti

Skip Bolen, whose work captures the feeling of carnival concerts in and around New Orleans, contributes to magazines including *Jazz Times* and *Downbeat*. His joyous photos of Mardi Gras with painted warriors and flaming torchlight marches, the contrasting images of the aftermath of Hurricane Katrina, and architectural landmarks in the city depict New Orleans from many angles. His use of natural light creates atmospheric images.

Luciano Rossetti, whose extensive portfolio captures live events, musicians, and characters at concerts across the globe, won the coveted Jazz Journalist Photography Award for 2021. His pictures are stunning, and he has been a jazz photographer for *Musica Jazz* and *JAZZit* magazines. He kindly donated some pictures to this book.

Jimmy Katz is an in-demand photographer, and his work has included wonderful shots of Sonny Rollins, Herbie Hancock, Pharoah Sanders, Ornette Coleman, Jamie Cullum, Diana Krall, Joe Lovano, and Ron Carter. Katz also won the Jazz Journalists Association photography award in 2006.

Other photographers include Urszula Las, Guy Le Querrec, and Tom Collins; their work enriches articles, brings books to life, adds detail and explanation. A good photographer can reveal, according to Evan Parker when discussing Guy Le Querrec's work, "details that we didn't know ourselves."

## JAZZ CONNECTIONS

IT IS APPARENT that jazz has its own culture but interacts with many other areas. The cross-pollination of ideas, incentives, inspiration, and performance affects other arts. Not all jazz venues just put on jazz concerts. They may also host classical concerts or art events, so it is all connected. Jazz also has connections to other art forms, including boxing and hip hop, which might surprise, but there are clear parallels, particularly when the American situation is viewed.

## JAZZ AND THE SWEET SCIENCE OF SELF-DEFENSE

MAYBE BECAUSE BOXING and jazz both offer the chance to rise from poverty and escape the dangers of growing up in a marginalized community, there has been a solid connection between the two art forms for decades. The connections go deep, right from 1907 when pianist Eubie Blake was discovered playing in a brothel by world champion boxer Joe Gans who asked him to play at the Goldfield Hotel. Given this break, Blake went on to study composition under conductor and cellist William Llewellyn Wilson and became a celebrated musician.

A boxer has a team of supporters, but ultimately it is one fighter against another, and winning is the difference between unimagined fame and ignominy. It is the same for a jazz musician. You may have a great band, but what you do on your own will make or break you as a musician.

Both jazz and boxing involve performing in front of a crowd, the art of knowing when to come forward, when to hang back, and when to strike, presenting a character through your art, improvising, all characteristics of jazz—I mean boxing—no, jazz, both.

There are subcultures attached to both jazz and boxing. Some people attend events regularly, support particular players. In performances of both, you can sometimes see where things are going or be utterly baffled at the outcome. Jazz, like boxing, offers potential income to marginalized and often poorer community members. Like jazz musicians, boxers have used their art as a vehicle to speak out on civil rights and discrimination.

Jazz and boxing require expertise, cunning, and an anticipation of how others will move. Both require supreme control over the body, nerves, and judgment. There is communication between players, reflexive reactions, intuition, and response. Both need a game plan—either for the fight or for the solos. Each produces stars and those who fall by the wayside.

In both art forms, the audience can be captivated by an outstanding performance or walk away disappointed. The better you play or box, the easier it looks, but the discipline and training that go before are immense for both.

Improvisation is required in jazz and boxing, yet both are built around basic rules and concepts. It is the performer who puts these into order or disorder. Jazz players can be flashy; they can come across as withdrawn and distant, yet within a millisecond, they can become emotionally charged, their playing bringing them right up close—and this is how it is with many boxers. While they work out their plans, their moves, and figure out the end game, they need a moment of reflection, but then they unleash the things that make them great—the flash decisions, quicksilver reactions, and the sharp, devastating responses. In both boxing and jazz, a performance is never the same twice.

Jazz musicians, including Miles Davis, used to mix with fighters and worked out in the ring at times in Chicago and New York. Davis viewed boxing as a science and saw similarities to performing music, such as knowing which way a player might go next after making a move and understanding how to position yourself to make the most of the move you think he will make. He sparred as a way to isolate himself before a performance.

Matthew Shipp is a prominent New York City-based jazz artist. He received a commission for a text to go with a film project on jazz and boxing, premiered at the Walker Art Center. In his text, which originally appeared in the Sports Edition of *CAKE* magazine, and which he generously allowed me to quote from,

Shipp says, "Like free jazz can be, boxing is direct, visceral. There exist both jazz and boxing subcultures—historically, sports and arts have been strong alternatives to mainstream economics in the black community.

"To an untrained ear, jazz can sound crazy; to an untrained eye, boxing can seem mad—as the ear and eye become trained, one learns the complex patterns that underlie the boxing match or the jazz solo—the theater of Kinetic Gesture—a kaleidoscope of intelligent quicksilver action generates a structure of intense beauty. For the body becomes poetry in motion whether through a keyboard or in the ring—complex patterned action generates a poetic time and space—violent yet dancelike, uncivilized yet graceful, raw yet sophisticated.

"The old-timers always referred to a great improviser as someone who tells a story—a great boxer tells a story but not with words or notes but in a refined language of will and transposed aggression. These acts of self-expression—fighting and playing a musical instrument—a neurological dance—the placement of fluid reflexes that reaches into the rhythmic pattern of a deeper intensity of human motivation—is it madness? The jazz solo speaks about the beauty of the neurological system, for it must mirror what it comes out of."

Sugar Ray Robinson, a hugely successful boxer who competed between 1940 and 1965, forged relationships with jazz musicians and thought himself something of a singer, pianist, and drummer. He was respected by musicians including Billy Eckstein, Miles Davis, Dizzy Gillespie, and Lena Horne. For jazz musicians, boxing offered them an additional connection to their audiences. When Robinson's career finally waned, he tried his hand at music. His name got him gigs, but audiences disagreed with his belief that he could play or sing.

Of course, there are differences. Jazz is more collaborative than boxing. A jazz player with inborn talent generally requires less teaching than an undisciplined boxer. Both, however, have to learn how to use their talents in a controlled manner.

Today, while the connections between jazz and boxing persist, hip hop, rap, and grime also connect in a contemporary way to young people.

George Foreman famously summed it up when he said, "Boxing is like jazz. The better it is, the fewer people appreciate it."

# HIP HOP AND JAZZ

WITHOUT JAZZ, THERE would never have been hip hop. Hip hop exploded during the 1970s, while jazz was contributing some of the most creative and exciting music to American culture. Many young Americans, and particularly African-Americans, would have grown up with parents who played jazz in their homes, so the integration of syncopation, swung rhythms, and jazz patterns into their DNA was inevitable.

In the 1970s, instruments were not available to the young in the same way they were for early jazz musicians. Technology had moved forward, and even if the music was incredible, who wants to play like your parents' generation? The rebels of the 1950s and '60s who brought visceral, dynamic new ideas to music were now middle-aged elder statesmen. Young people needed their own identity. So, they made new music their way.

The reduction of instrument funding in schools led, inadvertently, to part of hip hop's character. Not having many instruments around, young people looked at what they could use, and they had records, turntables, and ideas.

Hip hop, like jazz, did not come suddenly out of nowhere. Like jazz, hip hop imbibed elements already in music around the people and brought them together to create something new. Elements of hip hop were around decades before it became a genre. In 1925 a performer named Earl Tucker used dance moves such as sliding and floats—later used in break dancing. In 1940 Thomas Wong used a speaker to create loud whumping, boom sounds, which people loved. James Brown used rhythm patterns that later became known as breakbeats—all elements that would be taken, along with jazz, to create the new music. So, just like early jazz, hip hop took elements from the music already surrounding the people making it.

Jazz musicians, including Miles Davis and Herbie Hancock, had provided signposts indicating change was happening and directing musicians toward hip hop. Hancock's *Future Shock* (Columbia 1983) linked music of the past effortlessly to music of the present. Hancock introduced scratching on the album, partly inspired by Malcolm McLaren's "Buffalo Gals" (Charisma 1982). And it was not just Hancock or Davis. Early hip hop artists like Grandmaster Flash sampled jazz and jazz-funk recordings. As a rich, largely instrumental, and variable music form, with palpable rhythmic patterns, jazz provided perfect sampling material. It also had many sound ingredients, providing a deep pool from which to fish exquisite samples.

One of the reasons hip hop became popular was the vacuum left in the music when platforms like MTV presented commercialized, inane music to young people. Jazz and R&B were virtually unheard on these platforms. Jazz players seemed to have either gone toward fusion and funk or returned to traditional jazz. But from Jamaica came new sounds with sensual, evocative rhythms. Based on jazz rhythms, but blended with Latin and African patterns, this music was attractive to young people, and the combination of mouth percussion, mics echoing from boom boxes, scratching, and the addition of sharp, message-laced lyrics gave people a voice while simultaneously connecting them with their roots, including the rhythms and progressions of jazz. The sexier jazz rhythms suited hip hop perfectly, and the blending in of jazz samples gave listeners a master class in jazz whether they realized it or not.

The similarities between the emergence of jazz and hip hop are evident. Both jazz and hip hop originated as street music, and the engineers of both were primarily African-American. Both provided a vehicle for people who felt disenfranchised and marginalized. Hip hop, like jazz before it, offered upward mobility. Both were a social response and had a significant influence on the cultural fabric of America and elsewhere. Hip hop artists like Tupac, KRS-One, and Kendrick Lamar have commented on social issues and incited activism.

During the 1970s, young American people felt America was letting them down. Through their music, they voiced anger, concerns, and hopes. One of the problems with music in the late 1970s/early '80s was the massive commercialization and "sanitizing." Punk changed from visceral, meaningful music into wishy-washy new wave. Funk became disco, and jazz went smooth in some places. It was all gentle music suited to dance floors. But many young people did not want this prettified version of music, and it did not speak for them. They did not want genres separated, boxed, and marketed to different sections of society; they wanted music for all. (They were more jazz than they knew.) And it started well before *Future Shock*.

Early hip hop records include The Last Poets' eponymous release in 1970 (Douglas Records), where they used spoken words over jazz music. James Brown's *The Payback* (Polydor 1973) fused funk with rap, and DJ Kool pioneered linking two records together with an instrumental middle section, where lyrics were spoken. In 1972, DJs, including DJ Hollywood, began adding powerful lyrics over disco hits. These spoken lyrics over music became known as rapping. The history of rap music and hip hop go hand in hand. Both include other elements such as DJing, MCing, turntablism, scratching, and beatboxing. By 1975 more artists were using lyrics rather than melody as their vehicle for expression. They included Grandmaster Flash and his partner Mean Gene, whose little brother, known as Grand Wizzard Theodore, began scratching on records and later perfected "needle drops." In 1977 "crews" formed, including the Rock Steady Crew in the Bronx and the MC crew in Harlem. Other crews included the L-Brothers crew (Grandmaster Flash, Mean Gene, and others) and Black Hippy Crew, with Kendrick Lamar a key member. By 1979 hip hop had become part of America's street music but also provided commercialized rap for discotheques and dance halls—records like "Rapper's Delight" by the Sugar Hill Gang (Sugar Hill Records 1979) and "Oops Upside Your Head" by the Gap Band (Mercury 1979) were fun and commercial—and still come out at Christmas parties. In 1981 Debbie Harry "rapped" on Blondie's hit "Rapture" (Chrysalis 1981) and referenced Grandmaster Flash in the lyrics. The history and rise of hip hop are well documented, and by the early 1980s it was established as a separate genre. It was also used to express concerns, and in 1982 Grandmaster Flash and the Furious Five released "The Message" (Sugarhill 1982), which described the realities of inner-city life. This and other tracks validated rap as a voice for the marginalized in the same way jazz had in the early twentieth century.

In 1980, saxophonist Luther Thomas—known for his membership of the Black Artists Group (BAG), who united free jazz with dramatic theatrics, released *Yo' Momma* (Moers Music) with Dizzaz (Dizzazzsters Group), which was probably the first jazz-rap record released commercially.

During the late 1980s, a hip hop collective known as Native Tongues formed. They fostered a positive image and study of African history. Members included trios De La Soul, the Jungle Brothers, and A Tribe Called Quest. Releases included albums featuring saxophonists Pee Wee Ellis and Lou Donaldson, bassist Ron Carter, pianist Duke Pearson, trombonist Fred Wesley, and vibraphonist Milt Jackson. Carter's style of bass playing was perfect for the new, emerging music, with its thunking, solid rhythms, and he was sampled on several recordings. In 1991 he played on A Tribe Called Quest's *Low End Theory* (RCA 1991), which blends jazz with hip hop. Each track on *Low End Theory* featured a jazz sample. For example, Tribe used jazz legend Ron Carter on bass and sampled Eric Dolphy's "17 West" (from the album *Out There* (Prestige 1961)).

Carter was persuaded to contribute by his son, a hip hop fan, who reassured him of Quest's noble stance. Incidentally, Quest were led by Q-Tip, who grew up in a household where both parents collected jazz records. De La Soul sampled Ahmad Jamal's "Swahililand" on *Stakes Is High* (Tommy Boy 1996). The track was also sampled by The Game and RedmanImage

In 1988 the Jungle Brothers united with Native Tongues to produce *Straight out the Jungle* (Idler), which included elements of jazz, house, and Afrocentric music.

That same year, hip hop group Gang Starr sampled Dizzy Gillespie's 1946 track "Night in Tunisia" (RCA/Victor) on "Words I Manifest" (Wild Pitch 1989). In 1991, Dream Warriors featured a sample of Count Basie's 1967 "Hang On Sloopy" (Brunswick) on their "Wash Your Face in My Sink" (Island), while Freestyle Fellowship, a hip hop group from LA, used rhythmic vocals over bebop-infused tracks on their 1991 album *To Whom It May Concern* (Sun Music).

In 1993, Miles Davis's last recordings were released posthumously with samples and loops added by producer Easy Mo Bee as *DooBop* (Warner). Davis had, as ever, been aware of musical trends and sought out a hip hop producer for his final recordings.

Hip hop also appealed to younger jazz musicians. Alto saxophonist Steve Coleman recorded *A Tale of Three Cities* and *The Way of the Cipher* (RCA 1995) with his Metrics project. Metrics featured several hip hop artists, including lyricists Sub-Zero, Kokayi, Utasi, Shahliek, Black Indian, and Black Thought alongside Coleman, Andy Milne on piano, Reggie Washington on bass, Gene Lake on drums, Ravi Coltrane on tenor saxophone, Michael Wimberly, and Josh Jones on percussion, Ezra Greer and Duane Sarden on samples and dancer Laila.

A trend developed for bands to sample Blue Note recordings made during the 1970s. Organist Lonnie Liston Smith's career was revitalized when his music was sampled on "Talkin' All That Jazz" by Stetsonic (Tommy Boy 1988). In 1993, Digable Planets used samples of jazz musicians including Don Cherry, Sonny Rollins, Art Blakey, Herbie Hancock, and Rahsaan Roland Kirk on their *Reachin' (A New Refutation of Time and Space)* (Pendulum/Elektra), and in 1993, UK band Us3 secured permission to sample the Blue Note catalog, and this led to the 1994 release "Canteloop," which sampled Herbie Hancock's jazz standard "Canteloupe Island" from 1964 when Hancock was part of Miles Davis's Quintet (from the album *Empyrean Isles* (Blue Note 1964).

In 1994, Branford Marsalis led the Buckshot LeFonque project. It merged jazz with hip hop, funk, R&B, and rock. Collaborators included rapper Uptown, hip hop producer DJ Premier, DJ Apollo, Frank McComb, jazz bassist Reggie Washington, jazz trumpeter Russell Gunn and trombone player Delfeayo Marsalis. The name was a play on Buckshot Le Funke, which Cannonball Adderley used on the 1958 recording *Here Comes Louis Smith* (Blue Note). In 1993, saxophonist J. Spencer released *Chimera*, and in 1995 *Blue Moon* (both on MoJazz), which united jazz and hip hop.

Conversely, hip hop artists have played alongside established jazz artists and recorded crossover albums. Stetsonic, from Brooklyn, performed on stage with a jazz band and Public Enemy performed at the 2008 Montreal Jazz Festival—to the delight of fans.

The rapper Nas released *Illmatic* on Columbia in 1994, which featured samples of jazz trumpeter Donald Byrd. Nas's father is Olu Dara, a jazz cornetist, guitarist, and vocalist.

Hearing samples of jazz musicians led hip hop fans to seek out the original recordings and musicians, creating an accessible link to the past for young people and a connection with the young jazz musicians now playing. In 1994, Gang Starr's Guru sought out many musicians who had been sampled in hip hop recordings and brought them into the studio to play across the top of hip hop beats and top vocalists. This four-volume project, which ran until 2007, involved different jazz musicians, including trumpeter Donald Byrd, saxophonists Branford Marsalis, Courtney Pine, and organist Lonnie Liston Smith, alongside hip hop artists including MC Solaar, Common, and DJ Premier.

In 2005 jazz trumpeter Roy Hargrove released *Hard Groove* (Verve), featuring vocalists Common and Erykah Badu. This recording helped show that jazz artists were in tune with what was happening on the contemporary scene and that hugely successful hip hop artists were content to play alongside jazz musicians.

Just as jazz reflected social changes, hip hop did this too. In 2008, when Barack Obama was a presidential nominee, the hip hop community released several supportive tributes, and when Jay-Z headlined Glastonbury, hip hop gained genuine respect.

Any doubts about jazz's relevance to hip hop were vanquished when Robert Glasper's "Black Radio" series, begun in 2012, recorded with his electric quartet, featuring Snoop Dog, Badu, Common, Mos Def, Lalah Hathaway, and others. Glasper and other prominent musicians like Chris Dave and Mark Guiliana grew up during the height of hip hop's popularity but refused to be labeled. They wanted to connect music across genres. There is no doubt that hip hop features as part of the language of modern jazz, and the beauty is that it offers both schools of musicians increased freedom to blend genres and play with influential artists.

Alongside hip hop is jazz rap, where strong vocal lines are placed across the top of jazz instrumentation—bass, trumpet, saxophone, and sometimes percussion. Mixing spoken word with jazz had been done since the 1940s when DJs, including Daddy-O Daylie on WAAF, WAIT and WGN, added spoken lyrics over bebop jazz recordings. Jazz and hip hop are entwined both in the circumstances of their origin and their rhythms.

From Eric Dolphy to Herbie Hancock, Ahmad Jamal to Ron Carter and Branford Marsalis, jazz people are in hip hop, and the two genres are so intertwined as to be inseparable. As the elder sibling, jazz was here first, so hip hop lifts from jazz rather than the other way around. Hip hop has brought many young people to appreciate jazz. Maybe it should be renamed jazz-hop. It is a tradition to have a DJ play after a jazz gig in some clubs, and they often play hip hop to the same audience. Hip hop connects musicians and audiences of today with past jazz masters, and a hip hop master looking for samples will probably call first at the rich store of jazz.

To quote Fergus Hall again, "Hip hop has a strong presence in contemporary jazz culture, from the original compositions of jazz artists, such as Robert Glasper or Takuya Kuroda, to international artist Christian Scott performing a Jay-Z song or Berklee jazz students jamming a Kendrick Lamar song. These are hardly comparable to classic jazz standards, such as 'I Got Rhythm' by George Gershwin, yet they have been openly adopted into the repertoire."

Kendrick Lamar shot jazz into the mainstream with the album by American saxophonist Kamasi Washington in 2015, *The Epic* (Brainfeeder 2015), which he produced. Lamar had featured Washington on his album *To Pimp a Butterfly* (Top Dawg Entertainment/Aftermath Entertainment/ Interscope 2015), which led to considerable curiosity about Washington. Lamar also featured Robert

Glasper. Soweto Kinch's acclaimed *Nonagram* (Soweto 2016) contains powerful jazz-based music alongside hip hop influenced songs and hard-hitting modern street music. These jazz-rooted players are attracting a new audience along with bands like Polar Bear, GoGo Penguin, Elliot Galvin, Mike Casey, Daniel Bennett, and many players tuned into the kind of music their peers want to see and hear, creating a new wave of interest in music with jazz at its roots.

Many artists blur the line between jazz and hip hop, including Gary Osby, Flying Lotus, D'Angelo, Jason Stein, and more. With the improved technological connections, the know-how of marketers and video makers, hip hop has transcended jazz in popularity worldwide and brought a whole culture of clothes, art, dancing, and writing.

I would add, as a caveat, that hip hop, like jazz, is still changing. Like jazz, there is hip hop music that is "decade identifiable." The hip hop of the 1980s is different from that of the 2000s and today. Both kinds of music relate closely to their audiences and remain connected with them.

In late 2021 the hip hop artist Common appeared in Ronnie Scott's Jazz Club in an impromptu performance alongside trumpeter Theo Croker. Mike Vitti of Ronnie's told me they discussed the links between jazz and hip hop.

Of course, there are differences between jazz and hip hop. Jazz does not need words, while hip hop often relies on powerful vocals or poetry. Hip hop came about with a lack of instruments; jazz came about when instruments were readily available. To play jazz, the need to improvise is key, while this is less true in hip hop, although it happens in freestyle hip hop.

Jazz's cross-relevances to hip hop and boxing are just two areas where the influence of jazz has had ramifications beyond the music itself and crosses generations and art forms.

Modern classical music is influenced by jazz, as is popular music, rock and roll, R&B, and several other genres. The simple construct of jazz is attractive and makes it accessible—yet the creativity is also appealing to people who want to use the simple components and put them together in complex ways. Whatever genre it links with, the result is still jazz, but jazz with additional character.

# CHAPTER 6

## *Political jazz*

WHILE MUSIC ITSELF is apolitical, musicians aren't. Through jazz, musicians have echoed protest and political challenges, and jazz musicians have used their position and music to underline political messages.

As far back as 1912, W.C. Handy's "Memphis Blues" was originally written as a campaign song for Edward Hull, who became mayor of Memphis. In 1939, Billie Holiday performed "Strange Fruit" about the lynching of black people. Written as a poem by a Jewish teacher, Abel Meeropol, the song reveals the uncomfortable truth of racism at the time. Holiday's label, Columbia, was wary of releasing it, so Holiday convinced them to give her a short-term release to record it on Vocalion Records. Holiday's first performance at the integrated Café Society was a powerful statement with incendiary lyrics and dramatic presentation. As Holiday's final notes faded, the spotlight went out. When it came back on, Holiday had vanished—perhaps indicating what African-Americans felt was happening to them.

In the 1950s, concert promoter and record producer Norman Granz organized a touring show called Jazz at the Philharmonic that included Dizzy Gillespie and Ella Fitzgerald. Granz required promoters to guarantee no segregation of the audience. If Granz saw signs separating the audience at other events, he was known to remove them himself.

Back in 1945, Parker's "Now's the Time" had already insisted the moment had arrived for social change, and by the late 1950s, bebop became the voice of black America. They and others who could see the injustices of society were calling for freedom, and jazz expressed it better than words.

In 1957, under orders from the Arkansas governor, Orval Faubus, the National Guard prevented nine African-American girls from attending school in Little Rock, Arkansas. The incident became known as "Little Rock Nine." Faubus refused to capitulate, even though the law upheld integration in schools. After initially refusing to step in, Eisenhower finally charged the US army with protecting the students. Faubus promptly closed all schools in Little Rock. In

1959 Charles Mingus released *Mingus Ah Um* (Columbia), which included "Fables of Faubus," a reaction to the event. Tellingly, his record label did not include the full version of the song, feeling it too incendiary. Mingus had a reputation for speaking out, and one can only imagine the effect his acerbic rendering of the number with its clear message, mention of the Klu Klux Klan and the ridiculous idea of not allowing integration in schools would have had on those in the audience.

John Coltrane was deeply affected by the civil rights movement. He initially preferred Malcolm X's views of the separation of blacks and whites but later aligned with Martin Luther King (MLK) Jr.'s belief in a peaceful and more diplomatic resolution. Coltrane was producing music that challenged traditional jazz; he was adored by fans, inspired by religious belief and proving a light to many. As simmering discontent rose to the surface, jazz reflected the unease and became unsettled and dissonant. Coltrane was sharp enough to know that in his music lay power. He was deeply moved by the murder of four African-American girls in the KKK bombing in Birmingham, Alabama, in 1963. Two months after the event, he took McCoy Tyner, Jimmy Garrison, and Elvin Jones into Rudy Van Gelder's studio and recorded "Alabama," later released on the album *Live at Birdland* (Impulse 1964). Coltrane and MLK Jr. developed mutual respect, and Coltrane performed eight benefit concerts to support MLK's cause. Incidentally, when "Alabama" was included in John DeJohnette's 2016 album *In Movement* (ECM), sons of the original artists who recorded the number played—saxophonist Ravi Coltrane (son of Coltrane) and bassist Matthew Garrison (son of bassist Jimmy Garrison).

In the mid-1960s, deep-seated political issues surfaced and received jazz royalty attention. In 1963, the Congress of Racial Equality (CORE) organized two benefit shows featuring prominent musicians and journalists at the Five Spot Café in New York City. The event attracted Ben Webster, Eric Dolphy, Paul Bley, Ron Carter, Zoot Sims, and other musicians. Along with the National Association for the Advancement of Colored People (NAACP) and Student Non-violent Coordinating Committee (SNCC), CORE was a leading civil rights group, and the event gained powerful support. This was shortly after Dr. King delivered his "I have a dream" speech in Washington and just a month after the Alabama bombing.

In 1964, Nina Simone sang in Carnegie Hall. One song, "Mississippi Goddam," highlighted racial inequality as she worked in powerful words of protest at the treatment of marginalized people into its catchy, uplifting rhythms.

To the authorities, these jazz people now presented a problem. They expressed unease with American society in their music and had ideas they might change things or inspire others. The young, influential people attracted to jazz revealed flaws in the picture America had painted of itself. The musicians spoke out, and even their record labels seemed unable—or unwilling—to control them.

On the other hand, commercially, the music was generating income for the coffers of both commercial organizations and the tax vaults of the American government. The musicians seemed untouchable because of their high exposure and increasing financial muscle. A few drug busts here and there and taking their cabaret cards away when they overstepped the mark did little to dissipate their potential to cause uproar and embolden others to demand change. Morally they were challenging to shame and motivated more by their craft and a desire for harmonious living than money. Added to this, they were mainly black musicians who showed the inequality of American society to the embarrassment of its constitution.

The dilemma was, how to shut them up yet keep the support for jazz? The answer—mooted by Hazel Scott's husband, congressman Adam Clayton Powell Jr.—was to give jazz official approval. Voice of America—America's government media—labeled it "America's Official Music." Respected musicians were sponsored by the US State Department as "jazz ambassadors" and traveled to the Middle East, Eastern Europe, Asia, and Africa with a mission to demonstrate that America was integrated and civil rights upheld.

The irony of the tours was not lost on the musicians, and while they did wonders for the exposure of jazz to the world, they also created difficult situations for the musicians. While the musicians played to new audiences, advocating American values, their publicists might have neglected to state that many of these great musicians being fêted in foreign countries still faced discrimination in some parts of America. It was a poisoned chalice. Help spread jazz but at what cost to the truth?

In 1965 when Louis Armstrong was on tour in Denmark, he watched TV images of civil rights marchers in Selma, Alabama, being beaten by police and was horrified. He apparently told reporters, "They would beat Jesus if he was black and marched. Maybe I'm not in the front line, but I support them with my donations. My life is in my music." These remarks made global headlines. The same year, Armstrong was in Berlin, his first concert in the Eastern Soviet Bloc. He refused to be drawn on questions about events back in America, but people were wrong if they thought Armstrong would stay silent. He had his music. He had not included his song "Why Am I So Black and Blue?" in his repertoire for several years, but for the Berlin concerts he brought it back, slowed the tempo, and changed the words to put his message across. He actually substituted one word—"white" for the word "right"—but he changed the meaning of the song and the message to those listening was clear.

Duke Ellington believed jazz could empower progress toward equality and his faith seemed to drive everything. Even before the rise of the civil rights movements, he was, in his quiet manner, playing his part with contracts that stipulated he would not play in front of segregated audiences, and he rented entire train wagons when touring the southern states of America to protect his band from segregation laws. In 1941 he wrote a score for a musical, *Jump for Joy*, which challenged the traditional representation of black people, and his 1943 track "Black, Brown, and Beige Suite" told the story of Negros' supposed gradual integration in America. Its subtext of the creation and Adam and Eve (as Voola and Boola) is a parable of the history of Negros in America. They become brown, beige but never white. Ellington played at civil rights events and wrote music to commemorate the centenary of the abolition of slavery. He wrote a series of songs reflecting the experiences of African-Americans as *My People* (Contact 1963).

In 1966, there were violent riots when mobs of white people tried to prevent African-American children from attending schools in Alabama. Ellington played "King Fit the Battle of Alabam" at all his summer concerts that year in support of Martin Luther King Jr., and his later work of 1973–4, *Three Black Kings*, was dedicated to MLK. Ellington worked to uphold the position of black people and called jazz "African-American classical music."

Ellington and Armstrong were respected musicians who had long careers in the public gaze. You may wonder why they and other musicians were not more outspoken or did not take part in more civil rights marches and events. The answer lies in their intelligence. They probably achieved more by having long, successful careers—which cushioned them from media attacks or having trumped-up charges brought against them—than if they had issued explosive statements or got themselves arrested or barred from performing. As it was, they asserted their right to uphold the goodness in society and call out civil rights issues while remaining in the public eye and on the right side of the authorities—just.

Armstrong had pulled out of a tour in 1957 when Eisenhower initially refused to send state troops to protect the Little Rock students, saying he could not support the US constitution abroad if it were not upheld at home. Today, jazz musicians like Sonny Rollins and Wynton Marsalis show by their lives and how they treat others that they believe in their life choices, faith, justice, and live in such a way as to encourage others to follow.

The debt potentially owed by the world to the jazz ambassadors is difficult to assess, apart from the obvious fact it helped more people love jazz music. The goodwill generated toward America was significant—but maybe it goes deeper. In 1962 Benny Goodman visited the Soviet Union and played a concert attended by Nikita Khrushchev. Six months later, the Cuban missile crisis happened, and perhaps the goodwill generated by the jazz ambassadors affected the outcome more than we dare believe?

Press reports tell of dramatic encounters between audiences and musicians in countries behind the Iron Curtain and far-flung places like Asia and the Middle East. The jazz ambassadors tours worked well as part of America's cultural diplomacy because, while the Soviet Bloc responded by sending touring ballet companies, orchestras, and other cultural "weapons" to the world, several of their key performers defected to America—re-enforcing the idea that America was better than the Soviet Bloc as a place to live and thrive.

There were surprises too. Dizzy Gillespie's tour to the Middle East was successful, but audiences were surprised not so much at the mix of black and white players in the orchestra but the presence of female musicians, including trombonist Melba Liston and vocalist Dottie Salter.

Some jazz musicians felt they could serve best by going into politics or becoming activists. Alan Greenspan, who played clarinet and saxophone with the Woody Herman Band and Stan Getz and studied at the Juilliard School from 1943–44, served five terms as the 13th chair of the Federal Reserve, first appointed by President Ronald Reagan in August 1987 and retiring in 2006. One of Greenspan's bandmates, Leonard Garment, also went into politics, becoming Richard Nixon's special counsel.

The late, great Hugh Masekela (1939–2018) suffered persecution and banishment from South Africa because of his political beliefs and activities. He used to tell a story about how he was a white man who fell into the sea in Liverpool, floated around the world through oil slicks, and ended up in South Africa with his skin now black from the sun and the pollution. He was still the same man inside, but he was treated terribly when he returned to his homeland because he now looked black. Masekela was never a man to take lightly. When I was reviewing a concert and speaking with his agent by email, Masekela suddenly joined the conversation, taking over from his agent and gently arguing with me about an aspect of the music. He was encouraging and warm, but emphatic he was right (he probably was).

Other jazz musicians who have entered the political arena include Latin Grammy winner Susana Esther Baca de la Colina, who became Peru's minister of culture in 2011, Canadian jazz pianist Tommy Banks, who became a senator for Alberta from 2000–2011, and of course, who can forget that Dizzy Gillespie was going to run for president in 1964? His cabinet would comprise eminent jazz musicians, and one of his first acts would be to rename the White House the Blues House. Barack Obama did this for one day in 2016 to celebrate National Jazz Day. Obama enjoys jazz music, and I was privileged to get permission to use several parts of his National Jazz Day speech as the opener to one of my books.

Today, musicians become politicians too. Trumpeter, producer, and composer Raynald Colom is part of the elected party of a small town called Santa Eulalia de Riuprimer in Catalunya, Spain. I asked him why he went into politics, and he told me, "My reason is basically to help focus on culture and education for the young, creating programs about music in schools. We are currently implementing a music school in the town. Spain has a big deficit in culture in general. I first got interested in politics fifteen years ago when I spoke with trumpeter Wallace Roney and saxophonist Antoine Roney (brothers). They asked, 'What are your thought on music and politics?' That gave me a lot to think about and led me to what I am doing now." Colom told me that only about three percent of the government budget in Spain goes to the arts. In the UK, parliament has an all party committee, which has, as its aim, to support jazz music.

Jazz is collective music. Individuals make up the bands and ensembles, but they rely on the people around them and their reactions. It is a natural unifier and can galvanize people for a common cause. Often at a gig you will hear musicians discussing current events, atrocities, or even something comical in the news with their audience.

Jazz and politics differ in many ways, of course. Some musicians find politics dull and meaningless and party politics unappealing. Political parties follow a manifesto; jazz does not. Jazz offers people the chance to contribute, and debate is live and ongoing. Jazz has used technology to connect and share information with others worldwide, which has been especially important in recent times with the Covid-19 pandemic. Most politicians connect on a more local level, and information is not shared despite the available technology. In politics, conversations are rarely public; in jazz, they nearly always are.

Today, jazz is mainly apolitical, and in reality, it always has been. Hip hop artists have primarily taken on the mantle of jazz-influenced protest songs as a listen to tracks such as "Alright" from the album *To Pimp a Butterfly* (Top Dawg Entertainment, Aftermath Entertainment, Interscope Records 2015) by Kendrick Lamar will attest. It is the musicians who play and take up causes that politicize it. The music takes no sides in anything, has no views, but expresses the inner emotions of the player. The upshot is that whatever your political views, jazz today has no time or respect for them. Conservative, left, or right-wing, the jazz groove has room for you and however you want to express yourself.

## INSIDER POLITICS

OF COURSE, AS well as broader politics, jazz has its internal politics. There are the pushers, the ideas people who want things to change right now. They have plans to make things happen—they lobby politicians, push for fairer royalties from streaming companies, and align with specific bodies. All this is fine and healthy, and debate is always welcome—and usually lively among jazz people.

However, there are bullies. People who want things done their way or not at all. Success for them or no one. They will crush others, uphold their friends and ignore anyone who does not comply with their views. Unfortunately, these people's motives are often not apparent until they get themselves into a position where it is difficult to deal with them without becoming embroiled in public spats yourself. They are often clever enough to play the right cards until they reach a position from which they can bully without being challenged. Some are educators; some are leaders of small cohorts, gathered together under labels that promise members success or "exposure" but only serve to highlight the work of the "leader."

It might surprise you to learn that within this beautiful music, such people exist, but on the other hand, as I have said before, jazz reflects society, so it should not be shocking that a few miscreants creep in under everybody's nose.

The damage bullying can do to a musician is massive. Very few people speak out for fear of public humiliation or embarrassment, loss of work, or being seen as a bully themselves. From my discussions with many musicians, there is no single area of bullying. It is often not about race, culture, or gender; it is simply a matter of a sense of power that the bully feels. It is, thankfully, a relatively minor problem in jazz, but a problem nonetheless and an area most people would like to see disappear. When someone with a large following or in a powerful position deliberately posts misleading information about a musician, writer, or anyone online, it is hard for the lesser-known person to challenge them because they will be outnumbered. It is a little like a playground, and social media plays its part. I had not intended to give bullying much coverage in this book. However, when I put the question "Has anyone experienced bullying in jazz?" to musicians, the response was more significant than expected. Here are just some examples.

One musician told me he was thrilled to be invited to be part of a youth initiative. However, almost as soon as he arrived, the atmosphere felt toxic. He felt he was bullied and observed the bullying of others. The uber-competitive leader fueled the highly competitive atmosphere. There were favorites and those who hardly got a look-in. The leader made fun of band members' names if they weren't English-sounding, and his treatment of guest musicians was appalling. Oddly enough, rather than members speaking up and calling out the bullying, it encouraged some to bully as well. This created a very clique-like feeling of the leader and the favored few. The leader then left suddenly. He was replaced by a man who was intimidated by some of the orchestra members, who pushed for solos and refused to take his leadership seriously. They had learned well from their previous leader. Another change of leader saw someone in charge who demonstrated strong leadership skills, which got the best out of musicians without resorting to intimidation. The quality of the playing and the atmosphere improved immensely.

The point made by this musician is that many young musicians passed through this orchestra, as it was one of the leading youth jazz initiatives in the UK, so for years, a large cohort of top UK jazz musicians learned to achieve by bullying. They saw respected leaders do it; they learned well, so it should be no surprise that they exhibit bullying behavior further in their careers.

In another example, a musician told me of his experiences with a group formed at university. The leader filled the band with his friends, expecting them to work extremely hard. He was demanding both of their friendship and professional playing, so there was a blurring of the relationships. He constantly insisted that people were available. If not, he abused them verbally. At first, the band worked hard and did a lot of rehearsing, gigs, and touring for little to no money (as is the case with many original jazz projects). Emotional bullying and abusive verbal behavior intensified when band members prioritized other work or relationships over the band. "Banter" would result in personal revelations told to him in confidence as a friend. Jokes would be at their expense. Comments on their ethnicity or sexual partners were termed "just banter." In time, it became customary for the band members to "banter" with each other, making rude comments and jokes, but they began to feel uncomfortable. The musician told me he thought he was getting sucked into an unhealthy place. Eventually, he left the band.

Another musician was part of a band with a couple of top thirty hits, and they provided music for a film track. The band played around fifty gigs each year, with the leader taking around £30,000 for each performance. He paid the band members—many who had remained loyal for years—£150 per gig with no expenses. After five years, the band members got together and demanded modest improvements, which were granted.

However, Coronavirus came along, and lockdowns meant gigs were scarce. The band members asked what was happening and, after two weeks' silence, the management team informed them they were all sacked. They did this by WhatsApp! They had been loyal, put up with the band leader's tantrums, his verbal abuse, and his refusal to attend meetings in person.

However, Coronavirus removed the "carrot" he had of offering more work, so band members felt they could legitimately leave without the prospect of losing money. They now had time to go and find alternative sources of income and plan for the future. Later, WhatsApp messages asking them to return to the band were ignored.

Another musician told me this story. "A small but superb local Italian restaurant used to host a weekly jazz jam. Area musicians would come out to play, try out new material, and enjoy the menu and the camaraderie. Unfortunately, the drummer, who was also bandleader, succumbed to cancer. Two of the band members agreed to co-host. The pianist, while accomplished, went out of his way to play louder, take longer solos, and criticize the other player publicly. His goal was to push out the co-host. It got so bad the musician finally walked. The pianist got his wish and his solo spot. Then the establishment was bought out by new owners, and the guy lost the gig. Karma, maybe?"

Internal politics can sometimes be complex, and it can be easy for a writer, musician, or PR executive to offend someone with an innocent statement or comment. However, luckily for jazz, most appreciate the value of open conversation, and often when things appear to be escalating, the voice of reason will prevail. Many times, a heated discussion after a gig will result in drinks all round and a discussion of the performance—much better for everyone.

I hear from far more musicians who discuss the often-unexpected support from fellow musicians, writers, reviewers, and tutors. One lady told me, "My tutor was great. I was a bit of a smart-arse at music college. I had always won festivals and come top of classes—you know that kind of thing. When I came to college, I met others as good or better than me, and I found it hard. I still felt I knew it all, though, so when I played a piece I had practiced to my flute tutor, and she criticized it, I had a bit of a tantrum. I told her to stick her flute someplace and stomped off. After a while, I came back, and all she did was place the music back on the music stand as if nothing had happened, take her flute carefully out of its case, and play the piece like a bloody demon. It was amazing—so different from my interpretation. When she had finished, she grinned and said, 'If you had stayed, I was going to suggest you try playing it along those lines. What do you think?' No point making, no comments that I hadn't played my best or stomped out the room, no embarrassing me in front of the others; she just wanted me to play my best. And I did. I practiced and practiced, and next semester I had the chance to play the piece solo, and that tutor was in the audience. I played it along her lines but with my own twist, and she stood up—gave me a standing ovation. That is the kind of tutor I want to be."

The vast majority of educators—and I would include those on stage as well as college tutors—encourage those following. I have seen leaders of quartets, small ensembles, and orchestras give young musicians a spot, a chance to shine, and even on stage you can see the clear guidance provided by veterans to newer players with small hand gestures or movements of the head. I saw one quartet with a young saxophone player where the leader (drummer) directed the new member to come forward for solos, go back to allow others to take center stage at other times, and so on. Once, the lad tried so hard to merge into the background that he almost fell into a cupboard, but it helped because the leader and audience laughed with him and encouraged him to get back up and play, which he did. He was learning stagecraft, and it was a pleasure to watch.

Some experienced musicians will play with those newer to the scene and, if it feels right, they will step aside and happily allow them to shine—they feel neither threatened nor that these new players will take their place, and they view them as an enrichment to jazz.

# CHAPTER 7

## *Women of Jazz*

IF ONE AREA in jazz remains frustratingly difficult to explain, it is the lack of female musicians. We are in the mid-2020s, and it is difficult to imagine an art form where fifty percent of potential contributors are silently banned. Yet, it takes a keen observer to find the women of jazz. Initiatives, support groups, outcries on social media, studies, proof after proof of misogyny, books, papers—all show the situation, yet the progress rate remains incremental.

## SO WHAT IS GOING ON?

EVERY TIME YOU sense progress, you see yet another poster for a festival lineup and play "spot the female musician." You might find fifteen out of sixty, or five, but you will rarely see more than fifty percent female performers.

It shouldn't be like this. There are more female students on jazz courses, more female tutors, writers, promoters, and record label managers. A look online will tell you there are many female musicians recording, touring, and creating fabulous music. So why are women not more visible?

I know of no men who would rather it stayed this way either. Most are as puzzled as I about the absence of female performers in jazz music.

We are nearing equality in medicine, engineering, STEM (science, technology, engineering, and math) careers, politics, education, and other industries. Nothing stops women from achieving the highest levels—the glass ceiling was smashed decades ago. Yet jazz remains behind other genres like classical music in this respect, and it is a shame because women bring a different take, new ideas and enrich the scene.

# IS ANYTHING CHANGING?

THE ANSWER IS yes. Although, on the surface, jazz still appears male-biased, it is experiencing a sea change. Female musicians are being appreciated and encouraged. Finally, after decades, they are recognized as a valuable asset, not included for political correctness, but a genuine treasure that jazz has, thus far, missed out on. Although women make up fifty percent of the population, until a decade or so ago, jazz looked about eighty percent male, but there are more women now, and while their number remains relatively small, and the change is at a snail's pace, they are changing the scene. Jazz has become richer, more diverse, and multilayered.

Seeing women on stage or in roles like managers, PR, record label bosses can inspire. Others can envisage themselves doing that as a career, and the rock, which took a long time to get rolling, is gathering speed.

# WOMEN OF JAZZ IN THE PAST

WOMEN HAVE, OF course, been part of jazz ever since the first jazz player stepped out to perform, but they have been in the background—supportive rather than leaders—and they were assigned that role from the start.

A few bucked the trend—like Sweet Emma Barrett of the Preservation Hall, who had her first hit at sixty. She did not attempt to be glamorous but could play any man into submission. Her impact was so significant that some of her music was inducted into the Library of Congress. I was privileged to be asked to write the essay to accompany this.

Mostly, women were singers, pianists, or worked supporting men, and they had to be of very strong character to become anything else.

There is no dressing it up, jazz was misogynistic and chauvinistic. But, while there are no excuses, there are explanations.

Perhaps we need to go back to the origins of jazz and find ourselves in the clubs of America during the 1940s, '50s, and early '60s. Decades ago, men usually played jazz in seedy clubs on the wrong side of town. To become a band member, you often needed to attend a cutting session, a jam session, or be asked by another band member to sit in and take a turn. Cutting sessions took place late at night, often in seedy venues, and were contests of physical prowess (last man standing got the place). Jazz became a boys' club, and women were viewed as sexy, ornamental, and useful, but not essential. There were female singers, an occasional soloist, and very few all-female bands. But women had few rights compared to men; they had only got the vote across all America in 1920 with some groups excluded, and certain industries were virtually closed to women. The role of women in the 1940s and '50s was as mothers, homemakers, and men went out to earn money, so for them to step forward as leaders was not easy.

There were some renowned female musicians—trombonist Melba Liston, harpists Alice Coltrane and Dorothy Ashby, saxophonists Valaida Snow and Elsie Smith, trumpeters Billie Rogers, Dolly Hutchinson, Edna Williams, and more, who held their own among the men, but it took a good few years before women became accepted as equal players. Even when bands employed women during the wars, their places were relinquished to men after the war was over. To give some idea of attitudes in the past, author and jazz critic Nat Hentoff apparently said, in 1979, "When I was in my teens, I went with some friends to hear Woody Herman's band, and there, in the trumpet section, was a woman. We looked at Billie Rogers as if she had three heads and marveled that she could even finish a chorus."

## And today?

THE DIFFERENCE BETWEEN the past and today has to do with acceptance and expectations. In early jazz, more attention was given to how a woman looked than how she played, and today, what is important is what she brings as a musician. Given there are so many incredible female musicians—Nubya Garcia, Camilla George, Camille Thurman, Mimi Fox, Brandee Younger, Ellen Andrea Wang, Melissa Aldana, Jane Bunnett, Silvia Bolognesi, Rachel Z, to name just a very few—why are they not more visible in jazz music?

To get a perspective on this, I asked musicians what they thought and if they felt jazz was near parity yet.

Vocalist, composer, and podcaster Nicky Schrire said, "Definitely not. The numbers simply aren't there, and too many people in charge make no effort to balance the scales."

Pierre-Emmanuel Seguin commented, "We are nowhere near equality; you just have to look at magazine coverage. The majority of bands are men only, and women's visibility is still extremely low. I just had a quick survey of women on the covers of jazz magazines in the past year: *Jazzwise*: 3, *Jazz Magazine*: 2, *Jazziz*: 3, *Downbeat*: 2. That's probably not representative of the coverage of women in jazz globally but still quite shocking. Being French, I'm particularly interested in *Jazz Magazine*. The two covers with women during the last twelve months were Abbey Lincoln and Billie Holiday. Before that, it was Aretha Franklin

(October 2018), Melody Gardot (January 2018), Dee Dee Bridgewater (August 2017), Diana Krall (May 2017), Ella Fitzgerald (Mar 2017), Nina Simone (Nov 2016), Melody Gardot (May 2015), Cassandra Wilson (March 2015), Billie Holiday (Jan 2015). Not a single woman who is not a singer since 2015."

Broadcaster and content curator Mike Vitti added, "I still see a mostly male-dominated genre. I think venues are working hard to bridge the gap when booking, but said gap has been so wide for so long that it's taking longer than it should. I know Ian (Shaw), and I work hard to balance our guests and music on the program. It's a real minefield and I'm a true believer in merit bookings. I've seen a good number of UK women breakthrough over the last eighteen months, and that's a good thing. Long may that continue."

Saxophonist and engineer Sam Slotsky said, "My sense is we definitely have not (reached parity). One heuristic I'd suggest is to ask players who their influences are. In my experience, women don't get nearly enough mentions here."

With the increased exposure of female jazz musicians and more awareness, behavior toward them should be respectful and mindful. Wouldn't you think?

Well, here are some recent examples, which might surprise you. You can decide for yourself if you think jazz is quite ready for the "equality" title.

A venue manager told me about one evening when they had an exceptional female saxophonist as a guest. He saw a note slipped under the green room door during the interval. It was from a patron, asking if the saxophonist might smile a little more. The manager did not pass it on but wondered if the patron would ask the same thing had the player been male.

Another woman remembered an occasion when she enrolled in a singing class. When the instructor saw her, he commented, under his breath but audible, about liking beautiful women around him. When she sang, he refused to offer any feedback, while he gave others

The chair and saxophone wait for the musician.

Photo credit: Luciano Rossetti

encouragement and support. Then he began mocking her, trying to lower her self-esteem. She contacted the college, who gave her an alternative tutor, and she found other women in her new class who had left the other one for the same reasons. There appeared to be no sanction for the tutor's behavior.

Sometimes, women have to be wary of more than just odd behavior. Sadly, there are still men who think they are the best thing since... well, I am not sure what.

One young singer told me she often gets asked to have drinks with pro-moters after a gig. They speak to the rest of the band and then ask her to wait and have "a little drink with them." She did once or twice when she was more naïve but found things got a little uncomfortable when it was just her and the promoter in the bar and she needed to get a taxi home. Sometimes they offered her a lift, and one even suggested they go on to a club. As the band leader, she just wanted to talk business, get home, and finish her day, but she often felt an undercurrent of the threat that they would not offer support and promotion if she rebuffed them.

Another singer hired a well-known jazz pianist to play for her CD release party in New York City. When he arrived at the club, she had to rebuff his advances several times. Eventually, he went into a sulk. Then, the barman came over and asked if she had agreed to a tab, because the pianist had ordered drinks, saying they were to go on her account. She refused to pay, and the pianist played for half the set and then simply upped and left, leaving her with his bill and to finish the set on her own. She realized it was because she had refused his advances and he had decided to make things difficult.

Interestingly, when the singer shared her story with a more experienced singer, she got handed a list of all the potential sexual predators to avoid on the NYC scene—or "predators, users, and assholes," as the more experienced singer called them.

A female saxophonist told me that she had a long-running tenor sax/piano duo gig in Berlin with a male saxophone player. When it came to the contract renewal date, he called her from out of town and asked if she could get the details from the club along with a schedule. The club owner told her, "Let's wait until your man's back in town; I am not talking business with you."

I ran a mini-festival in London and engaged fourteen acts to perform—a total of forty musicians and singers. One guy approached me and said, "Blimey, the women are taking over! So many in one day!" I checked, and the women were vocalist Carmela Rappazzo, drummer and vocalist Kitty LaRoar, vocalist Gg, trombonist Sarah Gail Brand, vocalist Deelee Dubé, and four of the musicians in bands were female—a total of just nine of the forty performers. I had not even thought about it, just chosen the best players for the day. There still seems to be the "wow" factor at finding yourself at a gig where the band leader is female. Not only that, but "double wow" if some of the musicians are also female.

A female trombonist had a review of one of her gigs, and the reviewer ended the piece by stating, "and the most amazing thing was the trombonist was a woman!"

Another woman told me that when she accepted a position in a music school's arts administration program, she was also putting resources and time into her career and advocacy projects, receiving well-deserved attention in return. For weeks, the group featured in the *JazzWeek* charts and toured nationally and internationally. One day, the musician received an email from the head of the jazz department at the music school asking her to remove "jazz pianist" from her email signature. Puzzled, she asked for clarification and was told she was using her position to succeed outside the college.

This man assumed that she got attention and accolades based on her position at the school rather than her hard work and dedication paying off. She found this, she said, a very bitter pill to swallow. She believes that she would not have been asked to remove the title from her email signature if she was male.

I had to smile when I looked again at her email, and there, at the bottom, as part of her signature among several accolades, is "jazz pianist."

I have lots more examples of disrespectful behavior toward women, and it is not all deliberate but rather a hangover from deeply entrenched attitudes. People are still reluctant to name names and shame poor behavior in public, but hopefully a time will come when they do not need to consider this because lousy behavior will be a thing of the past.

Educator and musician Pauline Black commented that the gig scene is "male-dominated, with a lack of role models in education and in particular instrumentalists. Things are moving, though, and great things are happening."

Black is correct; there is progress in some areas. As part or whole of their aim, many organizations have the advancement of women in jazz music in whatever role they feel happy in—playing, PR, managing, working for record labels, all areas.

We have laws against discrimination, non-equal pay, and misogyny, while not officially a hate crime, is considered such by many. Initiatives like Keychange, started in 2015, have got hundreds of organizations to commit to change and aim for 50:50 male: female performers at music events by 2022. There are supportive groups, including Women In Jazz, She Shreds USA, PRS Foundation's Women Make Music, Girl Plays Jazz, She Is The Music, shesaid.so, Sisters in Jazz, Tomorrow's Warriors Female Front Line, and more. Workshops, classes, and courses for female musicians are offered and designed to empower them and increase the presence of women in jazz. Yet, for all this, there remain areas that need further consideration.

Educators and researchers, including Vick Bain, Andrea Vicari, and Terri Lyne Carrington, have conducted research and introduced programs that have helped. I have talked to many musicians, managers, agents, and educators, and there seem to be several factors that go some way to explain why women remain the minority in jazz. They include:

- Choice of instruments in schools—female students are encouraged to choose "feminine" instruments such as flute, violin, oboe, or piano. They are unlikely to choose a tuba, trombone, or bass clarinet. One music teacher told me that if their daughter picks a trombone or tuba, many parents ask if they can switch to flute or clarinet, as they do not feel a big brass instrument is suitable.
- Many girls show an initial interest in jazz, and some join ensembles, but there is a significant drop-off in their late teens. The reason for this is unclear, but it seems girls prefer the traditional path of playing in an orchestra or small ensembles.
- Unsocial hours and safety issues—women are more likely to feel unsafe in late-night clubs, bars, and coming home from concerts. And women are more likely to have unwanted attention than men. Many women think this needs to change, and recent events, including rapes, murders and abductions, and an increase in spiking, do not help. To get home safely often involves the expense of taxis or arranging lifts with trusted people.
- Motherhood—many women take a career break to bring up children, impacting their professional lives.
- Touring—with fewer women involved in touring, they need different accommodation and can feel isolated due to a lack of other females.
- Fewer female role models. Many women cite male musicians as their role models, and more women would encourage others.
- A lack of opportunities for female musicians is an ongoing issue. Venue managers and festival curators comment on the scarcity of available female musicians.
- Career aspirations—many women feel they can't find opportunities, but the media does not give them the same attention as men.
- Negative connotations associated with being a female leader—women leaders may find themselves tagged as bossy, pushy, or forward.
- There is a perception of jazz as a male interest by audiences and the media, and there are still gender pay gaps.
- People still think women are less likely to take a solo or be adventurous (though observers of trombonist Sarah Gail Brand, saxophonist Nubya Garcia, or trumpeter Charlotte Keeffe might disagree).

# PROGRESS: HOW DO WE MOVE FORWARD?

I ASKED MUSICIANS if they had ideas on how we might progress to make things more equal.

Columnist and writer Lee Rice Epstein said, "It's not difficult; the thought required is minimal. At the same time, the labels most fêted by popular critics have an abysmally low percentage of releases by women."

Educator and manager Kate Llewellyn said, "For a start, women should never apologize for being great at what they do or for asking questions about equality. My gut feeling is that young people are more forthcoming and will make changes... we needn't be binary about how we tackle the problem. Inclusivity isn't just arrived at. If everyone has a different way of tackling it, that's okay, and we will all make small steps (or giant ones) toward more women appearing center stage in jazz."

In Chicago, young musician Thaddeus Tukes comments, "I think we're not there at all, but the hope is in the new generation of musicians. I can say, in Chicago, we young folks are being intentional about representation. The university recruitment helps too. I can think of three women I play with from DePaul's jazz program alone. We're getting more women musicians who aren't just 'the singer.' They are very serious about the music. It's quite a time on the scene right now."

Education remains a crucial area in getting society to adopt practices encouraging young women to pursue music, including jazz. Constructs about "male" or "female" start when we are young, in our homes, schools, and colleges. Representation is key. Girls would be encouraged if they saw more role models playing instruments and taking leadership positions.

More young people are coming into jazz education programs in America, but many urban and inner-city schools have little funding for jazz programs, so students tend to come from families wealthy enough to purchase instruments and fund lessons. Jazz has moved away from the communities it came from and into suburbia. In Berklee and other institutions, programs are in place to support less wealthy students. Educators need to understand also that young people are more interested in the new forms of jazz where styles merge—so some hip hop, R&B, as well as traditional jazz.

Leadership needs to come from the front, showing fairness and equality, and an example needs to be given by tutors, lecturers, musicians, conductors, and curators.

We should start early—be mindful of not directing girls toward instruments that are considered feminine but allow them to choose one which they feel drawn to. Same for boys—we should stop thinking of masculine or feminine instruments.

Festivals and venues need to seek to employ female musicians—at least until there is more equality. Together, we need to drive toward the day when gender will not influence whether you get hired as a musician.

# WOMEN-ONLY GROUPS?

WOMEN-ONLY INITIATIVES WORK to promote women solely—and opinion is divided. They include festivals just for female musicians, groups on Facebook that only women can join, and groups that create female-only organizations for women. Some think this is great. After all, as one guy told me, "We have groups for sax enthusiasts, drummers, and so on, so why not for women?" I was unsure if we should see women's groups in the same way as for "enthusiasts," but I knew what he meant.

A female musician told me she felt the groups were pointless because they a) fragment what is already a small genre, b) place divisions when things are improving, and c) re-emphasize the marginalization of women and make the groups feel elite, which goes against the ethos of jazz.

Vocalist and composer Nicky Schrire commented, "I loathe the 'women-only festival' or even the 'all women band.' True inclusion means equal representation on lineups and rosters that include both men AND women. An example of this is the recent WBGO Fall Preview Listing—still a majority of men due to the numbers being what they are. And the number of jazz artist rosters on managers' websites that include maybe one woman. Or how many jazz broadcasters are women on a station's roster? It requires thought to make sure things are not one hundred percent men. It's not difficult to do. But it does require awareness, and many people simply don't care to engage their brains in that way. Maybe they've picked another battle to fight, but gender equality in jazz is far from balanced."

I remain undecided about women-only groups. I can understand the views about fragmentation and other factors; I can also see that women may feel empowered if they, as a minority, have more women behind and supporting them. I believe groups that offer workshops for women, including dealing with harassment or unequal pay issues, are a good thing. I perhaps have a certainty that the jazz community will find a way to rid itself of gender issues and look forward to the day when women-only groups will no longer be necessary.

As many musicians say, perhaps we should stop thinking in terms of "brotherhood" or "sisterhood" and just think of "everyone."

# THE FESTIVAL OPPORTUNITY

LAST YEAR, AS part of my research for another project, I went through thirty UK festival lineups to see the number of males, females, and mixed acts. In every case, the number of female performers or female-led acts made up far below fifty percent of acts in each festival—with some only getting to twenty percent. The average was thirty-three percent (a third) of female performers, and for this figure, I took both female leads and mixed acts with at least one female in the group. When a festival increased in size, female performers did not rise in proportion but often fell. It became clear that the overall number of female performers in jazz festivals was small.

I spoke to festival curators and managers, and their reasons varied—from there were just no female musicians around to no female musicians had come forward when they asked around for acts—who they asked remained a closely guarded secret. Some said they sought female musicians but could not find sufficient experience or standard, and agencies put forward only men. I asked them if they knew about initiatives like the F-list (a list of over 5,000 UK-based female musicians with their instrument, experience, and contact details). Some did, some didn't, and only two had looked at the list even though it is widely available. I found it hard to understand why so few women were engaged. Most of the curators did say they were trying to improve things.

Increasing diversity has been something festival organizers have wanted for a long time. They explained that their audiences have grown and become more diverse since they included more female performers. They also get more women coming to events on their own—and this applied to organizers at smaller venues I spoke to as well.

More women on stage equals more female audience members, more families, and younger people, so it seems the female presence offers more than simply increasing the diversity on stage.

As an example of the work going on regarding diversity, Teignmouth Jazz and Blues Festival identified three key areas where work was needed—and not just on the female inclusion front. These were: the age range of their audiences, the few attendees or musicians from the BAME community, and the lack of female musicians.

They decided to tackle the issues proactively. They invited bands from London to their rural southern festival and sought bands that included different cultures, ethnicities, and women.

Ian Roberts, chair of the festival, told me the organizers were conscious that most jazz (and blues) musicians were male, white, and elderly, so they decided to seek out female-led bands and musicians. Saxophonist Roz Harding and other female musicians played in 2019, and the balance of male to female musicians rose from negligible to around forty-five percent—a massive change.

Roberts said, "More females meant gigs were female-friendly, and we noticed more women coming on their own instead of as partners of performers, so it affected the dynamics positively."

The festival also joined forces with a theater so they could pay higher fees to guest artists and hosted events titled "The Lady Sings." They got stars, including singer Kyla Brox, pianist and singer Odetta Adams, and singer-song-writer Gabrielle Ducomble. The events were highly successful and showed that attention to parity results in a positive outcome, not to mention kudos. Attracting global stars means a festival can prefix the coveted and prestigious "international" to its name as well.

Other festivals have also curated events to attract more female participants. In 2021, Guildford Jazz Festival themed several events around Women in Jazz and invited female musicians and writers to speak. Now, more festivals are aware of the need to be inclusive and cultural diversity is becoming the norm.

And the positive movement continues. A browse through Cambridge's International Jazz Festival and the Brecon Jazz Festival in 2019 showed over a third of the performers were female.

We must also take heart from the fact that jazz has made progress. Consider that in 1938 *Downbeat* famously published a piece that included, "Why is it that outside of a few sepia females, the woman musician was never born capable of 'sending' anyone farther than the nearest exit? It would seem that even though women are the weaker sex, they would still be able to bring more out of a defenseless horn than something that sounds like a cry for help?" and when Peggy Gilbert, a renowned musician wrote a piece in response, they published her reply but only after adding the derogatory title "How Can You Blow a Horn in a Brassiere?" Gilbert became known for her support of female musicians, and today the piece is cited as the height of misogyny. Thankfully, this kind of article would probably not get past the editor's eye today. Why? Because women are more powerful, noticed and making change happen—along with the fact that enlightened musicians consider music before prejudice for any reason.

Generally, there is a sense of growing awareness, and increased feminine presence both on and behind the stage is clear. These days no one gives a monkey about your gender so long as you can play.

We mustn't forget there are other communities in jazz too. The LGBT and non-binary communities, for example. Some musicians and jazz supporters are open about supporting LGBT causes. In contrast, others see anyone's sexual orientation as private, but they need to be treated with due attention and care like every community. It may feel like a minefield, but generally, we should make good progress toward equality if we are mindful and treat everyone the same.

There is still work to be done for jazz to be considered entirely inclusive. Only then, when there is complete equality, will we play, write about and discuss jazz regardless of politics, race, gender identification, or any other thing that might cloud our judgment, can jazz be said to be wholly inclusive. We are, apparently, working on it.

## INSTITUTIONAL AND INTERNAL BIAS

CHANGE NEEDS TO happen on two levels. Firstly, institutional, and secondly, internal bias.

Institutional bias we can tackle because it is tangible. We can look at laws, change them if they are unfair, look at education, try to attract more female students to study jazz, and increase the number of female tutors, to provide role models. We can give established female musicians higher profiles so women see others playing jazz and realize that could be them. We can think of ways to create a safer performance environment, such as afternoon concerts, and change childcare and pay laws to make them fairer.

Venues can provide facilities that suit men and women. Safety issues need to be taken seriously, and we can organize workshops to educate women on tackling problems like bullying or pay disputes. All this we can do, and the industry is doing it in different places.

Internal bias is far more difficult to change because we are trying to change entrenched views. Women need to change how they see themselves. They need to believe they deserve to be stars, see themselves as soloists, and exceptionally talented artists in leadership positions. They need to see other women being successful and think, "that could be me!" Yet still, women worry they are not as good as the men, and they might get laughed at. They worry about how to react when things do go wrong. They even worry about how other women will treat them. The days when women became vocalists because this was less likely to be challenged than if they played an instrument should be long gone. The mindset needs to change, and women need to expect to be among the greats of jazz.

Great initiatives are happening to redress the gender balance, and you can check out some of those listed at the end of the book. Many of these are helping not only women but men of jazz, and they are helping jazz modernize, connect with young people and show jazz as inviting, with no one on the margins (unless they want to be).

Naturally, over the years, the subject of gender equality has been one I have discussed with musicians. Their take is interesting and sometimes quite surprising. Some believe progress needs to be measured because audiences need to evolve as well. The behavior toward women is so ingrained it could do damage if they try to force the issue. Others want things to change now, and if that means actively promoting women over men for a while, so be it.

The correct path probably lies somewhere between rapid change and slow progress. Some areas need targeting, and editors, for example, need to look at their content and if it can be perceived as being heavily weighted in favor of male writers and artists. Magazine content and covers need to show more women, reflecting reality—that they are here. This area, too, is showing signs of change.

# ANY OBJECTIONS?

SOME MUSICIANS HAVE expressed concern that if stages are flooded with female performers because quotas are encouraged—such as Keychange's vision of 50/50 parity, with fewer women in the first place—the quality is likely to be lower. I do not believe they need to worry. The quality of female performance is exceptional in all countries—Taeko Kunishima, Ellen Andrea Wang, Sheila Jordan, Georgia Mancio, Elise Morris, Ginetta Vendetta, Jane Bunnett, Terri Lyne Carrington, Silvia Bolognesi, Hannah Horton, Arema Arega, Isabel Sorling, Melissa Aldana, Camille Thurman and so many more. These and many more talented women could easily shine on any stage in any arena if promoters and curators would only look for them.

Some initiatives are clever and resolve problems in one sweep. The F-list (a list of over 5,000 female musicians, their genre, instrument, and location/ contact details) has negated the cry of "I can never find a female musician" in the UK, and it is freely available. One list, no excuses. Now, venues and festival managers can achieve parity with exceptionally talented women performing alongside men on an equal footing.

Gender equality will also dispel the myth of jazz being male-dominated and misogynistic. Nearly every musician says talent should get you the gig, not your gender. Given the number of talented female musicians now available, and with more on the rise, this should over time produce a scene stuffed with talented people.

Bringing the rest of the population into jazz has enriched it beyond the wildest dreams of most musicians. Collaborations between musicians of different genders bring new ideas and more experience to the table. There are incredible female musicians on the scene. These include those mentioned above, plus saxophonists Cassie Kinoshi and Camilla George, harpist Brandee Younger, multi-instrumentalist Emma-Jean Thackray, violinist Regina Carter, bandleader Esperanza Spalding, and many others. They join the ranks of established female musicians, including pianist and composer Carla Bley, saxophonist Jane Ira Bloom, guitarist Mimi Fox, and band leaders Toshiko Akiyoshi and Maria Schneider. They, in their turn, joined a lineage including saxophonist Vi Redd, guitarist Emily Remler, trombonist Melba Liston, vocalist and pianists Mary Lou Williams and Marian McPartland, band leaders Ina Ray Hutton (International Sweethearts of Rhythm), Ivy Benson, and Lil Hardin.

Despite obstacles, women are on the rise. Many women are in positions of influence and power in jazz; they are everywhere, from authors, columnists and reviewers, radio, PR companies, and managers of venues and musicians. Women run radio stations and host programs, including those on the US's increasingly influential Jazz Bites Radio. They hold managerial positions in record companies, with all the influence that has.

We should be at the point where male and female jazz musicians are on equal footing. It should be about the music, what you bring and whether you can perform well. Over 500 organizations from more than thirty-five countries signed a Keychange pledge that aimed for equality by 2022. It started as a European talent development program but also decided to tackle the issues surrounding gender inequality in the music industry. An ambitious project, it describes itself as "a pioneering international initiative which transforms the future of music while encouraging festivals and music organizations to achieve a 50/50 gender balance by 2022. Keychange aims to accelerate change and create a better, more inclusive music industry for present and future generations." The 2022 aim was ambitious, and we are nowhere near that in many areas yet, but it demonstrated a willingness to reach parity and raised awareness.

Only recently, the current situation was rather neatly put by composer Sam Eastmond when he saw a poster for a big band gig with male musicians. He reacted thus:

"One of the first things I saw this morning was a post advertising a big band gig, comprised entirely of men. This really pissed me off. The contemporary big bands I listen to are mostly run by women; others have kickass women in them. The point is, for me, music should be representative. It should contain voices and experiences and look outwards. Only hearing one facet of this is just boring. Great musicians are out there, but if fixers only book from a small, self-perpetuating pool, then they get overlooked. Anecdotally I've tried to get women (who are better than me) booked as subs only to find out not as good well-connected men got the gig. I want my music to reflect a community, and I'd like women to be in my community. With all the opportunities men have."

Women are sold a lie that jazz is not a viable career. It is, and there is an increasing number of women who have chosen to be jazz musicians and are making it work. With their continued presence, I think the improvement we need will happen. However, jazz, as we know, has its way of doing things, but without women, who would keep the boys in check?

# CHAPTER 8

## Speaking freely

### THE MODAL BRIDGE

JAZZ MUSIC WAS built around accepted frameworks with improvisation. The improvisation could become complex, but the framework remained essentially unchanged for many years.

Musicians became bored, improvising over the same chord sequences, playing around the same patterns. What felt comfortable for some felt like a creative prison to others. It took radical thinkers to do something different. It was to ideas used by past composers, including Ravel and Debussy, to which players turned—modal playing.

Modal playing uses sections where the mode (key or idea) changes with each section, usually to a related key but sometimes to a non-associated one, which can inject surprise. Some numbers are built around a few chords (e.g. Miles Davis's "So What"), but the player's modal usage and improvisational skill can make them feel complex and exciting. Chords are used, but the improvisation around them gains the main interest. "So What" is crafted around six chords, four in the melody section and two in the solo. Sections are built around different scales, such as the Aeolian or Dorian, which automatically introduces variations and intriguing differences, even in standards. Some musicians changed the ABBA or ABA pattern to AABA or AABBA, varying the solo sections and allowing many changes within a number. Modal jazz is popular because you can make it as complex as you want, or keep it more straightforward, so the demands on players can be less than with bebop.

Jazz would probably not have made the jump from traditional to free if there was no modal bridge for them to cross, linking traditional and free-playing styles. Without this step, the change might feel too radical. The modal style opened up possibilities; it explored each musical idea, and with more exploration, the freer the playing became.

During the 1960s, players began to push further away from traditional concepts by introducing harmonics to enable them to move between chords and scales in rapid and sometimes surprising ways. Pieces like Davis's *Milestones*, with "Cannonball" Adderley on alto sax and Coltrane on tenor sax responding to Davis's trumpet with twists and turns within the original mode, laid a template for modal playing, which led toward free jazz. To get a feel for modal playing, try Davis/Evans' "Flamenco Sketches" on *Kind of Blue* (Columbia 1959), Coltrane's "Spiral" and "Naima" (from *Giant Steps* (Atlantic 1959)), Bill Evans' *Waltz For Debbie* (Phillips 1962), Roland Kirk's *Rip, Rig and Panic* (Verve 1967) or Joe Henderson's *Inner Urge* (Blue Note 1966), which has a title track of almost twelve minutes of creative and beautiful modal jazz.

Asked to list great jazz players, many include modal players because they pushed the boundaries of accepted musical concepts and introduced exciting and surprising changes, yet the music still held a deep connection to traditional composition, so it felt familiar. Because modal jazz was incorporated into performances by respected players, it gained legitimacy. These musicians provided models for those who followed, pushing jazz toward even less restrained playing. Today, modal jazz is intrinsic to many players' repertoire.

Free jazz was resisted more. When Miles Davis first heard Eric Dolphy, he is said to have described his playing as sad and ridiculous. Hearing free jazz in the early 1960s, some critics said it would poison the jazz world. In the early 1960s, *Downbeat* critics described Coltrane and Dolphy's playing as "nihilistic exercises" and "anti-jazz." Given a few years, however, things changed. Davis found freer playing liberating, as did Monk, Mingus, and many others. Many modal players ended up playing free jazz, adding another style to their musical toolkit. And again, caution should be exercised labeling players because many modal and free players also continued to play traditional jazz and bebop.

For it to be accepted, the new way of playing—and players—needed to be heard, records needed to sell, and it needed the backing of respected industry people. Some labels steered clear of free jazz because they viewed it as marginal music, but not Blue Note. Blue Note was established in 1939 by Alfred Lion and Max Margulis, with Francis Wolff joining in 1941. Initially interested in recording traditional jazz musicians, from 1947, the label included modern and freer jazz. The label recorded Monk, trumpeter Fats Navarro and pianist Bud Powell and gained free players wider recognition.

For players like Monk, having the support of Blue Note meant they could record music they might not have been able to otherwise. Lion decided when he first heard Monk play that he had to record him. Monk later went to Prestige and then Riverside, but Blue Note provided the exposure he needed. Blue Note also proved key to drummer Art Blakey, saxophonist Lou Donaldson, and pianist Horace Silver. The label enjoyed a reputation for recording artists who pushed musical boundaries. Saxophonists Wayne Shorter and Joe Henderson, trombonist Grachan Moncur III, saxophonist Tina Brooks and trumpeter Miles Davis recorded some of their most beautiful music for Blue Note.

The most famous moment (so far) for free jazz was when Ornette Coleman on saxophone, with Don Cherry on trumpet, Charlie Haden on bass and Billy Higgins on drums, played the Five Spot jazz club in New York in 1959 and introduced free jazz into their set, causing some audience members to walk out, some to stand open-mouthed and others to applaud. Some critics found it an abomination; some praised Coleman's bravery. Others had no comprehension of what Coleman was trying to do.

Coleman played with an astute awareness of the music: he added subtleties and inflections, and his phrasing is still matchless. He presented music with renewed complexity and largely ignored the rules by which most jazz players at the time were bound. He used rhythms instead of melody or chord sequences as just one option for advancing a solo. His disharmonies alarmed some musicians, but the ability to hit notes just a quarter-tone sharp or flat is, in fact, something that only an expert musician can do (intentionally).

For many, Coleman was the answer to a prayer. Coltrane, Rollins, and saxophonist Jackie McLean were soon playing free in performances. Many had been pushing against the door of free jazz, and Coleman opened that door.

Coleman, disregarding any critics, kept pushing. One of his recordings, *Free Jazz: A Collective Improvisation* (Atlantic 1960), involved two quartets, one channeled to the left speaker and one to the right, with each quartet playing unrelated free improvisation. From the left channel came Coleman, trumpeter Don Cherry, bassist Scott LaFaro, and drummer Billy Higgins, and from the right the bass clarinet of Eric Dolphy, trumpeter Freddie Hubbard, bassist Charlie Haden, and drummer Ed Blackwell. It is challenging to listen for the full 37:09 minutes, even for the die-hard free-playing devotee, because the brain begins to follow one strong riff only to have that riff usurped by another and another—until it merges into utterly free descent toward something close to musical anarchy. This is Coleman to a tee and is the kind of music he was ever pushing forwards, where musicians play entirely free. It might be an example of the limitations of playing altogether free, though, because, while the exploration may be fascinating to musicians, hearing so many disconnected sounds is disturbing for the listener. However, the recording remains hugely influential and a pointer for anyone wishing to experiment in free playing.

Coleman brought to public attention a way of playing that many musicians had practiced in small ensembles, studios, and jamming sessions for years. Some traditional players would have felt threatened by this new style of playing, so they may have given it more criticism than it deserved.

Ayler, Dolphy, Shepp, up to modern players including reedsmen Peter Brötzmann, Evan Parker, Anthony Braxton, Mats Gustafsson, Ken Vandermark, and Ivo Perelman, pianist/composer Matt Shipp, and many more might point back to that time in the Five Spot and say, "this is where the public learned about free jazz."

The free jazz movement spread and provided a scene for a school of European improvisers, including guitarist Derek Bailey.

Although recognizably based in hard bop, Jackie McLean recorded albums that clearly showed free playing as part and parcel of his repertoire. His albums *Let Freedom Ring* (Blue Note, 1962), *One Step Beyond* (Blue Note 1963), and *Destination... Out!* (Blue Note 1963) give indications where McLean wanted to take his music, and free jazz compositions were interwoven on the albums.

There is a line we can trace back. The free players had models before them—Lester Young, Charlie Parker, Coleman Hawkins, Frank Trumbauer, and others. These were improvisers who played primarily within traditional concepts but provided models for modal players, who in their turn provided a model for later free players. Hard bop provided another breeding ground for free players with its gospel and blues influences alongside harsh atonal sounds. Formidable talent emerged from the scene. Free jazz takes elements—a key, chord, or sequences, around which improvisation happens and deconstructs the structure of a piece and builds it again, with irregular tempo changes and harmonics creating anticipation and adding energy to the music, but you have to know the structure well to do this successfully. Classic rules are still discernable in how the keys modulate and progress.

Free jazz appealed to innovative players who found even bop and modal playing limiting. Its explosive, interactive style also suited reactionary musical responses to events in the world through music. It may polarize jazz lovers, but interestingly, more than any other part of the jazz genre, free jazz links classical with jazz. You must understand music and harmony before playing free jazz that makes sense. It has been called "new classical" and the "future of jazz" by players including Ivo Perelman. Exponents like Cecil Taylor were classically trained, so they understood how music was structured, and free jazz enabled them to explore those constructs further.

Many musicians, including Charles Mingus and Thelonious Monk, are not specifically associated with free jazz but, given the development that took place during their careers, embraced a freer style in their later music.

In the late 1950s, Mingus regularly asked players in his jazz workshops to improvise on his music, often referencing the political changes of the time. Titles such as *Pithecanthropus Erectus* (Atlantic 1956) included a completely improvised section in the title track, and "Prayer for Passive Resistance" (Mercury Records 1960) pushed beyond bebop's boundaries incorporating Mingus's improvisations with sudden changes of tempo, rhythm, and volume. He was influenced by Ellington, gospel, and folk music and never lost respect for those models, but nonetheless set off on a different path. First and foremost a master of his instrument, he brought the double bass to the fore of many ensembles through his innovative playing. People were used to the double bass providing the rhythm or a steady background gait supporting the front line. In Mingus compositions, it was often the bass that led changes in tempo. His technical ability to create effects is still unmatched.

Mingus used the collective format so often found in free jazz. He would gather musicians and outline sketches of ideas but give them no music, allowing them to play around the concept and fill gaps with improvisation. This meant he got a different result with different collectives, which demonstrates another aspect of free jazz—it evolves because of who is playing.

Thelonious Monk incorporated gaps, repeated phrases in different formats, and used disharmonic chords and improvised sections in places. Although not always recognized as a free jazz player, Monk undoubtedly influenced jazz musicians who followed, like pianist Bud Powell, inspiring them to improvise and play according to their heart. Many players of that era, like Mingus and Monk, had backgrounds set in traditional jazz and never entirely moved to completely free playing, but their music forged links between bop, hard bop, and free jazz.

Pianist Lennie Tristano was linked early in his career to cool, bebop, and avant-garde, but he was pushing way into free playing before most other players. Some of his music was considered so difficult to market that it was not released until after his death, which is a shame for jazz.

I have watched modern-day free-playing bassist John Edwards play for over forty minutes, his bass creating high, low, smooth, rough, elegant, and visceral sound pictures because of his knowledge of the strings, detuning and retuning, the body, arco (bowing), plucking and banging to get the deep drum belches from the body. It feels like several instruments are playing rather than just one bass, and the music is glorious, sensual, slightly bonkers but feels great. I have watched the People Band, with drummer Terry Day, saxophonists Davey Payne and Paul Jolly, guitarist and violinist Charlie Hart, and saxophonist Evan Parker with guitarist John Russell and bassist John Edwards work around an idea—perhaps a poem or a key change pattern decided before a set. It is incredible what they get from a series of maybe four changes repeated, swapped, and explored. Similarly, Brötzmann or Mats Gustafsson can rework themes in so many ways the original idea is almost forgotten until they return to it finally, letting you know they never, for one moment, lost track of where they were going.

Many players enjoy playing traditional and free jazz. Rather than limit their opportunities, free playing opens new doors.

For some die-hard traditionalists, free jazz is the devil in jazz music. They perceive the players as unschooled, lacking virtuosity, and playing unpracticed (spontaneously composed) pieces. Yet there is an increasing, if grudging, understanding that you first need to be an outstanding musician if you are going to tackle playing free.

One aspect of free jazz is how it feels to listeners. You can predict a piece's direction in many jazz numbers because the melodies and rhythm are set up by piano, bass, or drums. In free jazz, the soloists, for their part, may follow the lead from the rhythm section or ignore it, establishing a theme based on part of the chord sequence or a relationship only they have found to the concept so that it can throw listeners completely.

Arguably, most jazz musicians have played free at some point, just some more than others. Coleman may have made free playing public—brought it out from the wings to center stage, but many players already had free elements in their playing. Dave Brubeck's flourishes, and Lennie Tristano's precision and deliberate choice of dissonant chords offered elements that could be used in free playing. Cecil Taylor introduced emotion and complexity to free playing. He was also influenced by Archie Shepp and European musicians, who were exploring different ways of playing and, by the 1950s, had established a definite left stream of players. Out of these would come players, including Peter Brötzmann, Anthony Braxton, Steve Lacy, Evan Parker, Alexander von Schlippenbach, and Charlie Haden, who found free jazz an outlet for emotions and a vehicle for exploration.

Some written accounts concentrate on American players, but it was in Europe that free jazz emerged with incredible power. The European scene was better equipped for free jazz due to its immense diversity. Generally, it was more readily accepted there, possibly because Europe did not have such a strong history of traditional jazz. It was also the epicenter of post-war anger and embarrassment, so the visceral discharges found in free jazz suited the explosive emotions players felt at times. Some young German jazz players, like Peter Brötzmann, told managers they were Dutch to get gigs because Germans were not welcomed. Brötzmann explained that in the 1960s, musicians felt like kicking out against post-war European values and recriminations. They were also outraged by events in America like the civil rights marches, continuing racial inequality, and Vietnam. He said, "In the mid-sixties, it felt like a violent time. There were race riots in Detroit and Washington, Martin Luther King was stirring the conscience of Americans, and there were burnings of churches and people. In Europe, there was unease, and the generation after the war wanted an alternative society. Music was the main way young people could express themselves. Though the US lacked unity, there was in Europe solidarity between musicians. Maybe this was missing before, but Vietnam had a knock-on reaction in Europe. There was little trust in authority."

In Africa, too, free jazz became popular, with the Cairo Free Jazz Ensemble—an offshoot of The Cairo Jazz Band, formed by Salah Ragab and Hartmut Geerken in 1968.

Musicians from the original free jazz scenes of the 1960s are still playing today—Brötzmann, Parker, Han Bennink, Alexander Von Schlippenbach, Palle Danielsson, Armen Nalbandian, the Art Ensemble of Chicago, and others have followed, including Hamid Drake, Mark Cisneros, Dominic Lash, and Casimir Liberski.

The European and UK scenes had diverged from the jazz in America, helped inadvertently by the decade or so long dispute which prevented jazz musicians from crossing the Atlantic either way to play. When the Atlantic crossings were reinstated, the music on both sides had taken different directions. So, Europe took the jazz it had—and it had some impressive musicians and some American ex-pats—and developed it. The music imbibed influences from the locality, whether that was France, Germany, Italy, Denmark, Norway, or Spain—wherever the players found themselves.

The jazz scene in Europe also had input from Scandinavian musicians and other European countries' folklore. What Europeans did with America's greatest musical export was nobody's business. They added a touch of German anger after the war, a smidge of English reserve, and a lot of rebellion against austerity and restrictions during the 1950s.

It has to be said that the Europeans did not really respect the touring musicians from America. Europe did not have segregation based on skin color (though there were other forms of discrimination), so in many ways Europeans had the freedom to explore and push jazz to its limits in a relatively liberal setting. Across Europe were cohorts of musicians who came together to do just that, and this continues today with the European free jazz scene remaining perhaps the most diverse in the world.

European venues, including Jazz-Schmiede in Düsseldorf, the Chocolate factory in Berlin (Schokoladen), the Hot Clube de Portugal in Lisbon, and the Jazz Republic in Prague, that host free jazz enjoy a devoted following. London has a strong scene, and most free jazz players would compete for a place on the programs of Cafe OTO or the Vortex. I asked Mats Gustafsson, a prominent Swedish/Austrian free jazz saxophonist, why the UK scene is so strong. He told me, "Perhaps because the British remain quirky, willing to listen to new sounds and give people a chance."

The very term "free jazz" is a misnomer in many ways. It implies freedom from any structure, but music is, by its nature, structured. Peter Brötzmann explains, "No one can do exactly what they want. It is a dialectic process, and you have to be responsible. When you work with somebody or something, you make it your own even if you destroy the existing rules. It is always a dialogue between what you have in mind and what is possible. The language you use is based on the character of the person speaking—or playing."

Whether audiences are ready for change is crucial. It is presumptuous to expect an audience to suddenly appreciate music that deconstructs nearly every parameter they know and understand.

Parker, Gillespie, Monk, Mingus, and Coltrane all helped push jazz to new limits, and subtly, changes were happening. Long before Coleman, the stage was set. After Coleman, the door was left open, and since then, free jazz has developed beyond some listeners' wildest dreams or, as some traditionalists would say, their worst nightmares.

Yet, it is true there are times when an audience member might ask themselves of free jazz, "what am I listening to?" I have been to gigs where the vocalist has simply moaned and screeched into the microphone, or the drummer gave an extended "solo" of dusters being rubbed on the cymbals and feathers used to hit the snare. I have seen a pianist completely wreck a piano keyboard by bashing it countless times with an iPad, which was destroyed in the "performance." I have witnessed self-absorbed musicians make squeaking noises with balloons while being completely unaware that the audience has mostly left for the bar area. I have endured horrible sounds which have no relation to each other whatsoever created by players thrashing their instruments in ways no one intended. Those times, I wondered what I was listening to. Yet, I have also witnessed free jazz, which is divine, incredible, dynamic, music that carries the listener away and to a different place. I have seen players play with such intensity you could imagine paint drying with the force of their breath, and I have had the incredible experience of losing a sense of place and time because a player is making music so exquisitely beautiful. So, free players are at times treading a fine line where music turns to noise, related sounds turn to complete disharmony, and that place is just shy of the furthest extremes where serene beauty is found. The truly talented musicians can play free and keep the listener on the edge of rapture. Players today who play excellent free jazz include pianists Lars Fiil and Matt Shipp, saxophonists

Ivo Perelman and Colin Webster, drummer Andrew Liles, bassist John Edwards, trumpeter Charlotte Keeffe, the band Polyorchard, and many more.

Around the same time free jazz exploded, art was taking an improvisational route and literature became abstract. Many view free jazz as punk's predecessor because punk bands' even more anarchic, chaotic music took spontaneous composition, worked it into repeated verses, and added pop instruments. Ted Milton's band, Blurt, is an example of jazz-punk fusion. The music is glorious.

During the 1970s and '80s, there was an attempt to return jazz to a more controlled, predictable style. Few clubs booked free players, and those that did were small, generating little income. In Europe, the distances musicians had to travel to get gigs increased, and many began to find it challenging to play.

I asked Brötzmann once if he ever came close to giving up. He told me, "In society, to do something against the mainstream, you have to be aware that you have hard times to face and decide for yourself which way to go." He added, "It is important to use your own language. There is no other way to speak. If you switch styles, you can corrupt your language."

The difficulty for free jazz players to get gigs led them to create their own in what became known as the loft scene—small get-togethers with invited players and guests who could buy tickets; they were in tiny venues, houses, anywhere the players could meet up.

Manfred Eicher's label ECM, based in Munich, was important for free jazz, recording artists including the Art Ensemble of Chicago, Paul Bley, Lester Bowie, Ed Blackwell, and Don Cherry. Now many labels support free jazz players, including 33 Jazz, Edition, ESP-Disk, Not Two Records, Edgetone Records, and many others.

New music has always been slow to be integrated into the mainstream. We accept it and move on, looking for the next new thing. When Beethoven first introduced music with a different emphasis, it took people a while to understand or enjoy it, but now, Beethoven is familiar; Coleman sounds like blues with a twist, as our ears and minds become accustomed to it, change and tune in to new sounds. Free jazz is really just an extension of bop, modal, and an alternative to the familiar soundscapes. Even more than traditional jazz, it allows the expression of emotions—sometimes it is so profound it blows your mind, and after free jazz exploded onto the scene, jazz has never been the same—in a good way.

And jazz has evolved since free jazz. New players come all the time with new ideas. The use of technology, pedals, and sound effects has also added to the musical possibilities. With time, new ideas become integrated alongside traditional jazz. It is evolution.

# CHAPTER 9

## *Jazz family*

FOR MANY EARLY jazz artists, family life revolved around music one way or another. Marching bands, church, the sounds they heard around them from different countries: music was at the heart of daily life and celebrations. Jazz developed to became part of their DNA.

The love of jazz has passed down generations and affected the broader family of many musicians. A surprising number of jazz musicians began a dynasty, with children, grandchildren, and other relatives following them into the music.

I wondered if being part of a musical family meant music was an easy career choice, but musicians tell me they were never pushed into jazz, nor were doors automatically opened to them, although contacts may have been easier to make with other jazz players in the family. It just happened they liked jazz, and many have family members who did not choose jazz as a career.

As children, we learn our elders' values. Growing up with musicians in the family, young people get the chance to hear good music, and because they listen to it over a long period, they will hear it when they are receptive to it. I believe this is important because it is not a given you will like jazz just because your family plays it.

It may depend on whether your first experience is positive or not. I know people whose parents love opera or classical, but because the first time they heard it or had to sit quietly through a long concert was when they were too young to fully appreciate the music, it instilled a lifelong avoidance. Musicians have also told me they found some jazz unfathomable when they were very young, but the same piece had a different effect when they were older. One said, "*Bitches Brew* for me was inexplicable at eleven but revelatory at fourteen." Another, "I wasn't hip to Coleman when I first heard him, same with Bird, but I kept coming back to see if my ears were ready. I knew they were legendary for some reason. My ears had to evolve."

As small children, we are taught rhymes and nursery songs that are easy and repetitive. Later, young people may enjoy pop songs that follow easy patterns. They identify with the music their peers listen to and that music doesn't challenge. Some jazz played on the radio, and as background music, is boring, so the average young person is not exposed to good jazz unless they seek it out. If it is played at home, however, it is there for them when they are ready to be challenged or for that day when they find themselves tuning into it. If you grow up seeing your family play jazz and, what is more, see it brings them happiness—and income—you are probably more likely to listen to it.

Many people I have spoken with have made two journeys into jazz. The first is short and often not sweet. They find jazz complex and prefer the familiar formats of pop songs. But the next time they try jazz—especially if it is good jazz—they understand, and bam! They are hooked.

If you grow up with music, you get to see it being created. The jam sessions, the ideas mooted and played with, the coming together of different concepts and communication between players. You can get this, of course, from other places, but if you have it on tap, as it were, you are almost bound to drink some of it in.

People who grow up in jazz families also learn that you have to work and become technically accomplished to reach the high standards expected by audiences paying to hear you play or who buy your music. Encouragement can come in many forms—an insightful parent purchasing an instrument, a great teacher, or just being in an environment where picking up an instrument is easy and you have people around you willing to put up with the learning process.

Talent is a requirement and maybe growing up with music allows access to inner talents people may not realize they have. Many people could learn a subject or art by rote, becoming proficient. But it is having a natural talent and learning how to deliver and find your own voice which makes you unique. Many people learn an instrument or participate in other arts for years and make little headway beyond a certain level. They may be fine, but they are not great, and this is as true of jazz family children as it is for established musicians.

The life of children born to working musicians is a different one. Children are exposed to a different lifestyle from their peers from their earliest days. They might not see their parents much of an evening, or they may, as many have told me, accompany their parents to performances at a time when most children are in bed, some taking naps in the green room, or on the journeys to and from a venue.

Most musical families encourage but do not push their children into music. However, given the exposure, the opportunity, and the time spent hearing music, it is no wonder the upcoming generation is tempted to pick up an instrument. Of course, having a family member who is a musician may provide opportunity, but it doesn't guarantee anything. You need the dedication to apply yourself to learning the craft and rely on far more than your family name to get bookings.

One female executive of a record label whose parents were respected jazz musicians told me she had tried her hand at singing, and her parents encouraged this, but after a few gigs, she decided it was not for her and studied business at college—with their blessing. A few years later, she asked her father what he thought about her singing. He looked at her and, after some thought, said, "My darling, this I know. You are a terrific businesswoman." She knew she had made the right choice and loved her father for not discouraging her from finding her path in life for herself.

There is no better way to understand what it is like to have a musical family than to hear from those with experience, so I asked vocalists Laura Ainsworth and Selina Albright, singer/songwriter, producer, and radio broadcaster China Moses, and trumpeter, vocalist, and composer Benny Benack III what their childhoods were like, whether they felt it a duty or a choice to follow in their parents' footsteps. I also asked trumpeter Duane Eubanks what having his brothers in jazz was like.

Laura Ainsworth is the daughter of clarinetist and alto saxophonist Bill Ainsworth, who played with the Tommy Dorsey Big Band—a bop-hued collection of impressive musicians including Ainsworth, Vernon Arslan, Sid Cooper, Sam Herman, and others. Ainsworth Snr. recorded with Dorsey and also Tex Beneke and Ray McKinley's Big Band before that. When she was a child, Laura told me that her father was always on the road and somehow knew where to find the best food in every town—he was particularly partial to bread pudding. He played in showroom bands behind big-name stars, including Tony Bennett, Mel Tormé, Tom Jones, Marilyn McCoo, Billy Davis Jr. (5th Dimension), and others in Dallas and the Las Vegas Desert Inn. Ainsworth Snr. had a pilot's license and would rent small planes to fly to gigs. One particularly awkward landing led Laura to vow she would never get on a small plane again. Bill met his wife when he played with the Ernie Felice Quartet at the Tail o' the Cock restaurant in LA. A lady named Louanne Hall came in, feeling depressed that she didn't have a date, and it was her birthday. Though very shy, Ainsworth introduced himself to her, and later she became his wife and Laura's mother.

Laura says, "I often meet older musicians around Dallas who are still in awe of my dad. Trombonist Jim Milan is in his nineties and leads the Bucket List Jazz Band. Every time I see them, he tells anyone standing nearby that I'm the daughter of the greatest musician he ever knew, the only player he ever played with who never hit a wrong note. He used to be in Curly Broyles' group with my dad and Leon Breeden, one of his best friends, who founded the University of North Texas Jazz program. Jim said he dreaded every solo because the order always went Leon, Bill, then him, so he had to follow those two. He also tells of my dad writing extremely complicated big band arrangements in his head in the car on the way to a gig. He also used to do it at our kitchen table. A few years ago, my husband and I bought the 1955 house I grew up in, restored it, and I now have that yellow table back in the kitchen for inspiration. Dad was a prodigy and started with Tommy Dorsey at seventeen, but his big band days were long over by the time I came along. I grew up around great singers because he was the jingle session leader at PAMS and CRC by day, making sure every note and harmony was spot on (his nickname in the industry was "The Judge"). Then, at night, he was alto sax/clarinet player for Jerry Gray at the Fairmont Venetian Room. My mom would take me on the free band family nights to see him back people like Ella Fitzgerald, Tony Bennett, and Mel Tormé."

I asked Laura whether it felt natural to follow her father into music. She said, "Absolutely. I never thought of doing anything but music, theater and writing, while my sister went into real estate."

Laura then dropped into the conversation the fact she is third-generation jazz. She said, "Louise Upton, my grandmother on my mother's side, was the pianist in an all-girl ragtime band when she was a teenager. I don't know the group's name, but I know they played on a vaudeville bill with the California Sunkist Syncopators. She also started when she was only a teenager but quit early to get married. She kept playing piano but was forced to stop when she developed arthritis at only thirty-five. Very sad."

China Moses is the daughter of American singer Dee Dee Bridgewater and granddaughter of Matthew Garrett, a jazz trumpeter. She told me, "I was fortunate to have a very supportive family and two wildly artistic and encouraging parents. So much so that as soon as I expressed a desire toward the arts, they did everything in their power to make sure I had what I needed. I didn't really want to become the singer that I am today. I wanted to work in the arts but behind the scenes. I imagined myself as many things: a producer, a video editor, songwriter, coach. None of those things required me to get out on center stage. In the guise of therapy, my mother sent me on the weekends to work with her dear friend Jerry Lipkins. At his house, I started making demos. I was rapping; I really wanted to be a rapper. My father would always say I was a star and would be signed to Virgin Records. He would unfortunately not see that day, for he died a few months before I signed my first contract at Virgin Records, France. It was bittersweet. But how I ended up at that particular label when I didn't even want to be an artist was of my mother's doing. I was failing in school. She took a song I had been working on and played it for an A&R (artists and repertoire—people who found new talent for labels) guy. He thought I had a very particular and recognizable voice, but I couldn't rap.

"All that is to say that my parents, and their diverse entourage, were one of encouragement and love for the arts, a true definition of a tribe of people who make art with intention. They were also freethinkers, activists, militants, and lovers of life, so I think if I decided to become an accountant, they would have been fine with that, as long as I found a life, a way toward being content and fulfilled as a human."

Vocalist Selina Albright is the daughter of saxophonist Gerald Albright. Along with performing her own music, she has, since 1997, contributed to her father's projects and played with musicians including Joe Sample, Norman Brown, Marcus Miller, Dave Koz, David Sanborn, Kirk Whalum, Steve Cole, Boney James, Hugh Masekela, Chaka Khan, Will Downing, and The Temptations. I asked her what it was like as the daughter of a prominent musician. Was there was ever any doubt she would follow in his footsteps?

Selina told me, "Being the daughter of a prominent musician was unlike many other childhoods one would consider 'normal,' but I didn't know that because the experiences of my childhood created my definition of 'normal.' I interacted with celebrities other kids wouldn't normally have access to. I was introduced to nightclubs and concert halls as a baby and taught how to behave while my father was performing. I was brought along to countless recording studios where Dad would work and got to experience the practice and focus behind the development of his technical skills and unique sound firsthand. I was a proud 'night owl' when other kids had to be in bed by 8 pm. I was rarely allowed to get my clothes dirty because, as my mom repeated many times, I was 'representing the family every time I left the front door.' It was a lot of pressure, but it groomed me.

"My parents knew I had talent and promise as a musician as early as when I was just two, but they never forced me to become a musician professionally. Instead, they made sure that the necessary tools for all my interests were at my fingertips so that I could decide my passions freely. All I knew from the beginning was that I wanted to be my own boss whatever I did. So, I first prioritized finishing school, earning my degrees, and securing a backup plan. Then I searched my soul to find my true passions. I was determined not to be a 'starving artist.' Of course, when I felt the time was right to pursue music full-time, my parents were very proud and supportive! (And I still haven't missed a meal yet.)"

Selina gravitated to jazz because that was the music she was exposed to the most. She says, "From a young age, I heard my father's music regularly, and friends of the family would gift me jazz CDs—anything from Ella to Coltrane to Thelonious."

Benny Benack III is the grandson of Ben E. "Benny" Benack (1921–1986) who was a fixture at baseball games for many years, playing in front of the crowds attending Pittsburgh Pirates and Pittsburgh Steelers games. He led the Benny Benack Orchestra in swing and Dixieland jazz and was known as the "King of Dixieland." Benack toured with the Tommy Dorsey Orchestra and Raymond Scott Orchestra. Of Benack's three children, Peek continued the jazz line and performed as Benny Benack Jr., playing trumpet, clarinet, and saxophone. Peek's son, Benny Benack III, continues the musical tradition into the third generation and is an international soloist, playing alongside artists including Joey DeFrancesco, Aaron Johnson, Christian McBride, and others. Benny Benack III's mother, Claudia, is also a vocalist and accomplished musician. Benny told me she met his father in the Dodge Kids—a show band Benny Jr. used to run in Pittsburgh with college-aged students over the Summer. Benack says, "Three generations of jazz in my family and three generations of Benny Benacks... way cool!"

Duane Eubanks is the younger brother of jazz and fusion guitarist and composer Kevin Eubanks and jazz and fusion slide trombonist Robin Eubanks. His mother, Vera, was Kenny Baron's piano teacher, and his uncles were jazz pianist Ray Bryant and bassist Tommy Bryant. His cousin David was a pianist, and a cousin, Charles, is a pianist.

He told me, "Being raised in a musical environment is a blessing for a budding musician. You get to see firsthand what is possible if you are dedicated to your craft. My uncles, Ray and Tommy Bryant, have performed with Miles Davis, Papa Jo Jones, Lee Morgan, Curtis Fuller, Jackie McLean, and the list goes on. They would randomly visit my mom and offer musical information to us. To hear stories and to be able to ask them musical questions was an amazing situation to be in. Their willingness to share information and their ability to make a name for themselves made it a lot easier for my brothers to see themselves succeed musically. I personally got to see them all do well, and that is an amazing boost. I didn't have to read books. What was possible was right in my living room. I had total access to the vital information."

Many famous jazz names have family members with music in their heritage. Just a few are listed below, and not just sons and daughters. As you can see, jazz is a real family affair.

Pioneering drummer Warren "Baby" Dodds (1898–1959) played with Armstrong, King Oliver, and other leaders. His elder brother, Johnny (1892–1940), was a jazz clarinetist and alto saxophonist who played with Armstrong, King Oliver, and Jelly Roll Morton.

Bandleader, composer, jazz clarinetist, and saxophonist Jimmy Dorsey (1904–1957) had a brother, Tommy (1905–1956), a jazz trombonist, bandleader, and composer.

Brothers Hank, Thad, and Elvin Jones were jazz musicians. Hank (1918–2010) was a jazz pianist, arranger, bandleader, and composer, Thad (1923–1986) a legendary trumpet player, and Elvin (1927–2004) a jazz drummer who played with Mingus, Bud Powell, Coltrane, and Miles Davis.

Bud Powell (1924–1966) worked with Charlie Parker, Thelonious Monk, and Dizzy Gillespie. His father was a jazz stride pianist, and his brother was Richie Powell (1931–1956), who was just twenty-four when he died but already had achieved success as an arranger for Max Roach and Clifford Brown. He was killed along with Brown in a car accident.

Tenor saxophonist Gene Ammons (1925–1974) was the son of blues/jazz/ boogie-woogie pianist Albert Ammons (1907–1949), whose parents were both pianists. Albert was encouraged by local blues-playing neighbors in his hometown in Alabama, including blues/boogie-woogie pianist Pinetop Smith (1904–1929).

Miles Davis's (1926–1991) mother, Cleota, was a violinist and music teacher.

Standout jazz trumpeter and flugelhornist Art Farmer (1928–1999) had a twin brother, Addison (1928–1963), a formidable jazz bassist.

Edward Ayler (1913–2011), a semi-professional violinist and saxophonist, survived both his sons, saxophonist Albert (1936–1970) and jazz trumpeter Donald (1942–2007). The brothers were members of the same groups for several years, and Donald worked with Paul Bley, Elvin Jones, Sam Rivers, and many more.

Jazz pianist Kenny Drew Jr. (1958–2014) was the son of jazz pianist Kenny Drew (1928–1993).

As well as these, many jazz musicians we know today come from a line of jazz musicians.

Saxophonist Wayne Shorter had an elder brother, Alan (1932–1988). Alan was a free jazz flugelhorn and trumpet player (having switched from saxophone). He played with the Jackie Bland Band, and members included

Wayne. Alan recorded albums *Orgasm* (Verve 1969) and *Tes Esat* (French America 1971) as leader (reissued by Verve in 2004 and 2005). His style was free-form and beyond the understanding of American taste, though he found some success in Europe. When he was booed off stage one time, he is said to have shouted back at the audience, "You're not ready for me yet!"

Nat Adderley Jr. is the son of trumpeter Nat Adderley (1931–2000). His uncle was saxophonist Julian "Cannonball" Adderley (1928–1975). Nat Jr. is best known for his work with Luther Vandross. He produced many Vandross singles and seven of his albums, playing piano or keyboards on most of them as well as for other recording artists. He is a conductor and has worked with the London Symphony Orchestra, appeared in films and musically directed stage shows. Latterly he returned to his jazz roots, working on music that pays tribute to his father and uncle.

Four of the Marsalis brothers, Wynton, Delfeayo, Branford, and Jason, have followed in their father's musical footsteps. Pianist Ellis Marsalis Jr. (1934–2020) played with Courtney Pine, Irvin Mayfield, Nat Adderley, and his sons. Each son has carved out their unique place in jazz. Trumpeter Wynton is a composer and educator, and his work, particularly with the Jazz At Lincoln Center, has gained him international recognition. Saxophonist Branford has played with his own quartet, Art Blakey, Herbie Hancock, and hip hop and classical recordings. He is also known for playing with Sting.Trombonist Delfeayo has his Uptown Jazz Orchestra, has released many recordings, and produced others. Drummer Jason leads the 21st Century Trad Band and has played with Lionel Hampton, Joe Henderson, and more. Ellis recorded with all of his sons and often sat in on performances. I enjoyed seeing him play piano with Delfeayo's big band in New Orleans' Snug Harbor, where he played the second set of a three-set evening. I saw Wynton when he played with the Jazz At Lincoln Center Orchestra with guest Wayne Shorter at London's Barbican Centre.

Jazz drummer Denardo Coleman is the son of Ornette Coleman (1930–2015), one of the great free jazz players. When he was just ten years old, he joined his father's band, and Charlie Haden apparently commented, "He's going to startle every drummer who hears him."

Saxophonist Sébastian Texier is the son of bassist Henri Texier, who played with Randy Weston, Phil Woods, Lee Konitz, the Strada Sextet, and more. Sébastian has played on many projects with his father and albums by François Merville.

Vocalist and producer Pyeng Threadgill is the daughter of composer, arranger, saxophonist, and flutist Henry Threadgill. Her mother, Christina Jones, is a dancer in the Urban Bush Women dance group. Pyeng has performed at the Fillmore, Montreal, Clifford Brown Jazz Festivals, and many renowned jazz venues. She studied at the Oberlin Conservatory of Music and gained the Mellon Fellowship to study music in Brazil.

Drummer Antoine and vocalist Himiko Paganotti are children of bassist Bernard Paganotti. Antoine and his father sometimes even share the same billing.

Bass player Felix Pastorius is third-generation musician. His grandfather, John Francis Pastorius II (1922–2004), was a stand-up jazz drummer and singer. His father, John Francis Anthony "Jaco" Pastorius (1951–1987), took up the drums before switching to bass and becoming one of the most revered bass players in the world. Felix has played with Bobby McFerrin and tours with Jeff Coffin's The Mu'tet and the Yellowjackets.

Drummer and bandleader Clark Tracey is the son of jazz pianist Stan Tracey (1926–2013), a regular player with Ronnie Scott and Ted Heath. Stan was the house pianist at Scott's jazz club in the 1960s, and his later career saw him play with free jazz legends, including Evan Parker and John Surman. Clark and Stan played together in Fathers and Sons, with clarinetist John Dankworth and his bassist son Alec, whose sister Jacqui is a jazz vocalist (both children of Cleo Laine and Dankworth).

Jazz guitarist David Reinhardt is the grandson of Romani-French guitar player Jean (Django) Reinhardt (1910–1953). His father, Babik (1944–2001), surprisingly did not learn guitar from Django, who died when he was nine years old, but from his uncles, particularly Joseph, an exceptional rhythm guitarist. Babik was drawn to jazz fusion and visited America to play several times before his death in 2001. David has played many international festivals, and he dedicates many of his performances to his grandfather.

Saxophonist and clarinetist Ravi Coltrane is John Coltrane's son. John Coltrane's legacy was his music and that of his second wife, Alice, and his sons, John Jr., Ravi, and Oranyan. John Jr. was a promising bassist but was killed in a car accident when he was seventeen. Ravi's cousin, Steven Ellison, AKA Flying Lotus, is a record label owner, producer, rapper, and DJ. Oranyan started playing jazz with his brothers but has gone into trance and electronic music production. Many of his recordings feature jazz samples.

René McLean is the son of saxophonist Jackie (1931–2006), who played with Monk, Davis, Powell, Woody Shaw, and others. René is a hard bop saxophonist who has played with Woody Shaw, Hugh Masekela, and others. His grandfather, John McLean Snr., was a guitar player in Tiny Bradshaw's orchestra, where he played jazz and rhythm and blues.

Saxophonist Joshua Redman is the son of Dewey Redman (1931–2006) and dancer Renee Shedroff (1932–2016). Joshua was exposed to jazz, classical, rock, soul, Indonesian, Indian and African music, and many instruments. He began playing clarinet and switched to tenor saxophone at nine years old. Dewey Redman was a force within jazz music, playing with Coleman, Donald Garrett, Don Cherry, Charlie Haden, and Jane Bunnett. He was integral to Bunnett's recording *In Dew Time* (Dark Light Music 1988). Bunnett told me that Redman encouraged her to "be herself on her instrument and form a unique concept for herself"–which she did.

Jazz vocalist and songwriter Michelle Hendricks and vocalist Aria Hendricks are daughters of jazz lyricist, vocalist, and exponent of vocalese and scat singing Jon Hendricks (1921–2017). Jon performed with many jazz greats, including Count Basie and Duke Ellington.

Vocalist Claudia Solal is the daughter of Algerian jazz pianist and composer Martial Solal. Claudia has worked with Sylvain Kassap, Joshua Abrams, Phil Minton, Maggie Nichols, and many more and with her father.

Bassist Charlie Haden's (1937–2014) family used to play on the radio in their locality. Haden worked with Paul Bley, Archie Shepp, Keith Jarrett, Dewey Redman, Bill Frisell, Ginger Baker, and many more. All his children, triplets Petra, Tanya and Rachel, and son Josh, have had successful musical careers. Petra has become known for her eclectic and accomplished music. She uses her extraordinary voice to recreate instrumental sounds. She plays violin and has worked with Bill Frisell, Foo Fighters, Greg Anderson, and a long list of musical luminaries. Tanya is a cellist and vocalist, a member of several groups, and has performed with her sisters as the Haden Triplets. Rachel plays bass, drums, guitar, and sings and has performed with Beck, Todd Rundgren, The Rentals, and many more. Bassist and vocalist Josh Haden founded the group Spain.

Vocalist Ana Gracey is the daughter of saxophonist Barbara Thompson and John Hiseman (1944–2018), who led three pioneering jazz/rock groups. Since she was very young, Gracey has been singing and songwriting and enjoying a very successful career.

Vocalist Jeanie Bryson is Dizzy Gillespie's (1917–1993) daughter and has a successful music career.

Albert "Tootie" Heath is an American hard bop drummer. His brothers were bassist Percy (1923–2005) and saxophonist Jimmy (1926–2020).

Four out of Dave Brubeck's (1920–2012) six children went into jazz. Darius is a jazz keyboard player and educator; Christopher plays bass trombone, piano, and electric bass and composes, active in jazz and classical music. Matthew performs jazz and classical and plays cello, bass, keyboards and is a composer and arranger. Dan is a jazz drummer. Their mother was jazz lyricist Iola Whitlock. Brubeck Snr. was an influential jazz musician who changed how many people thought about jazz. His brother, Howard (1916–1993), was a composer and music educator.

Saxophonist Marcus Strickland's twin brother is E. J. Strickland, a jazz percussionist who plays with Ravi Coltrane.

The Bosman Twins, Dwayne and Dwight, are saxophone players, educators, composers, and arrangers who frequently record and play together. Their mother, Paula V. Smith, loved jazz, and their father, Lloyd Smith, was a sidesman for Count Basie and Ellington's orchestras.

Guitarist George Freeman had brothers hard bop saxophonist and NEA Jazz Master Earle "Von" Freeman (1923–2012) and jazz drummer Eldridge "Bruz" Freeman (1921–1996). His nephew Chico Freeman is a saxophonist, bandleader, and composer.

Acoustic bass player Marion Hayden's father, Herbert, is a jazz pianist, and her son Tariq Gardner is a drummer, educator, and composer.

Karriem Riggins is a jazz drummer and hip hop producer whose father Emmanuel Riggins (1942–2015) was a keyboard player, composer, and singer.

A three-generational jazz dynasty is the Batiste family of New Orleans. Norman Batiste (1929–2021) was a revered member of the Treme (6th Ward) community of New Orleans and a self-taught jazz musician, mainly playing the bass drum. Harold Batiste Jr. (1931–2015) was a composer, arranger, educator, and leader in the New Orleans community. Lionel (1931–2012) was a jazz drummer and singer who played the bass drum at the Square Deal Social and Pleasure Club in New Orleans. He inspired many jazz musicians. Alvin (1932–2007) was a jazz clarinetist; Milton (1934–2001) was a jazz trumpet player. Of the next generation, Russell is a drummer playing funk and blues music, Michael is a bass player who has performed with Jackie Wilson and Isaac Hayes. His son, Jon, is a bandleader (Stay Human), musician, and TV personality.

Saxophonist, clarinetist, and flutist Joe Lovano's father was Tony "Big T" Lovano, a barber by day and musician by night. Joe is married to singer Judi Silvano, and his brother Anthony is a drummer.

Jazz pianist, composer, and singer Karen Mantler is the daughter of composer, pianist, and bandleader Carla Bley and Austrian avant-garde trumpeter Michael Mantler. She contributed to her mother's recordings from a young age, and after attending Berklee, she continued to record with her mother and branched out with her own projects.

Saxophonist Claude Ngcukana's father was saxophonist Fezile Christopher "Columbus" Ngcukana. He was known as "Columbus" in his native South Africa because he constantly discovered new ways with music. He raised a family of musicians. Of his other sons, Ezra (1955–2010) was a saxophone player, Duke (1948–2011) was a jazz trumpeter and educator, Fitzroy is a vocalist, cultural activist, and poet, and Ray and Fana are singers.

Pianist Zoe Molelekwa is the son of jazz pianist Moses Taiwa Molelekwa (1973–2001). Moses played with Hugh Masekela when he was just fifteen. Zoe won a Hugh Masekela Heritage scholarship.

Saxophonist Alan Skidmore is the son of saxophonist James Skidmore (1916–1988), who worked with Humphrey Lyttleton, Kenny Baker, and others.

Jazz pianist and composer Michael Garrick (1933–2011) has a son named Christian, a violinist and professor of jazz and non-classical violin at three of London's leading music conservatoires. His brother Gabriel runs the Jazz Academy courses started by their father.

Finnish trumpeter Verneri Pohjola and trombonist Llmari are sons of bassist and composer Pekka Pohjola (1952–2008).

Drummer Gerry Gibb's father is vibraphonist and bandleader Terry Gibbs. Gerry became house drummer for the legendary Blue Note Jazz Club After Hours Band in New York and has worked with Alice Coltrane, Woody Shaw,

Buddy de Franco, Clark Terry, and John Hendricks.

Bass player Eric Mingus is the son of legendary bass player Charles Mingus (1922–1979). Eric has forged a career playing with musicians including Carla Bley and Karen Mantler.

So it goes on. There are more.

Guitarist Bucky Pizzarelli (1926–2020), who collaborated with many jazz greats, including saxophonist Zoot Sims and vibraphonist Red Norvo, has sons Mike, a bassist, and John, who is a guitarist and singer.

Jazz guitarist Grant Green Jr. is the son of jazz guitarist Grant Green (1935–1979), and jazz bassist Matthew Garrison is the son of bassist Jimmy Garrison (1934–1976). Composer Tayondai Braxton is the son of experimental improviser Anthony Braxton, and saxophonist Ted Nash is the son of trombonist Dick Nash.

Drummer T. S. Monk is the son of jazz legend Thelonious Monk.

Viola player, violinist, and composer Mat Maneri is the son of saxophonist and clarinetist Joe Maneri (1927–2009).

Guitarist, vocalist, and bandleader Casper Brötzmann is the son of free jazz titan Peter Brötzmann.

So, jazz, it seems, is in the DNA of many families—father, mother, daughter, sons, sister, brother, cousins. Yet each has their voice, presentation, and unique way of delivering their music. It probably helps that most of these musicians were exposed to jazz of the highest quality from very early in their lives.

It would be fascinating to be a fly on the wall in some of the conversations or family get-togethers and overhear ideas discussed, the arguments perhaps, the agreements on who plays what, when, and how.

Encouragement when young is a factor in the lives of many musicians. Other jazz musicians did not come from musical families but benefited from having people who encouraged them to follow their musical hearts. Eric Dolphy's father built him a studio so he could jam with others. John Coltrane's mother bought him a saxophone when he was sixteen. Thelonious Monk's mother got him piano lessons when he was six years old, and Bud Powell's father got him piano lessons when he was five. These people must have seen something in the children and wanted to nurture it.

A trumpet, a microphone and the music is played.

Photo credit: Luciano Rossetti

As a child, having musicians in the family means you have access to practice rooms, studios, and your family is more likely to understand that every musician has to go through the squeaks, skronks, warbles and scrapes before they finally begin to piece their music together and make beautiful noise.

Looking at jazz dynasties reveals something else. Many musicians today are a single generation from the greats, whose names we often hear, and many of the players who set jazz music alight passed only recently. Violinist and saxophonist Edward Ayler, 2011; pianist and composer Dave Brubeck, 2012; musician and singer Lionel Batiste, 2012; saxophonist Ornette Coleman, 2015; keyboardist and composer Emmanuel Riggins, 2015; saxophonist Don Rendell, 2015; pianist Ellis Marsalis, 2020; musician and bandleader Jimmy Heath, 2020; composer/keyboardist Chick Corea, 2021; pianist Barry Harris and trumpeter Ron Miles, 2022; all recent and only first- or second-generation jazz musicians. Jazz is young and still developing.

Like when you see a view of mountains in the near distance, you can imagine breathing in the cold, pure air; you can almost feel the wind on your face. You can't actually touch them, but you feel you might if you reached out your hand. It is the same with jazz legends. Their stories are told by many, and their influence is so significant still that they feel touchable, almost as if they are standing in front of you, and hearing them play brings them even closer. They are almost within touching distance.

Too often, jazz is depicted as historical music, but think about this. If he were still alive, Coltrane would have been ninety-six, Albert Ayler eighty-six; Charlie Parker was born only just over one hundred years ago in 1920. Then look at the incredible jazz musicians, many of whose names are as familiar today as they were four or five decades ago who are still playing: Wayne Shorter, Archie Shepp, Sheila Jordan, Pharoah Sanders, Joe McPhee, Marshall Allen.

The jazz dynasty goes on, with people coming in all the time, bringing new blood, fresh ideas, and often supreme talent. Gregory Porter, Robert Glasper, Courtney Pine, Jane Bunnett, Jane Ira Bloom, Mimi Fox, continue to produce great jazz, and the outstanding young musicians, relatively new on the scene but already making a name for themselves—Nubya Garcia, Laura Jurd, Esperanza Spalding, Cécile McLorin Salvant, Elliot Galvin, Melody Gardot, Julia Dollison, Brandee Younger, Camille Thurman, Kendrick Scott, Leo Pellegrino, and there are many more, some of them having musical parents, others not, but a new generation is growing.

The history of jazz spans over a hundred years—probably nearer two hundred, if we include the years before it was documented, and it is still being written. So, definitely not a music of the past but one we have only begun to develop, with a bright future—vibrant, full of life, and always welcoming new players.

## THE NEW GENERATION

IT IS NOT just because of family connections that young people are coming to jazz.

Venues are encouraging and offer platforms to new players. Many offer regular slots to music students to give them a taste of playing in front of an audience. Many veterans welcome young players into their band for part of a gig or even to sit in (play as a visitor) for a performance. For the venues, the veterans who pack the house are one thing, and the quieter evenings with newer or less known players are very different, but they know the value of kudos, and when some of the new people get famous, they will hopefully return—and pack the house themselves.

The tradition of the elders supporting newer players or the established artist encouraging another musician is extraordinary. I have seen Evan Parker play with young saxophonist Binker Golding, and Wayne Shorter exchanging experiences with Wynton Marsalis, and Clark Tracy encouraging Sean Payne—a young saxophonist who now leads his own ensembles. Inter-generational connections continue, and new ones are growing. That is jazz in a nutshell—it is simply what you bring to the table. If you are willing to learn and work hard, you are welcome.

Many jazz musicians regularly gig worldwide, keeping venues alive and maintaining the connection between jazz and its audience. Established musicians keep venues busy. These include New York bassist Mark Wade, saxophonists Tony Kofi and Daniel Bennett, clarinetist Adrian Cox, saxophonist and bandleader Ray Gelato, bassist John Edwards, saxophonist John Butcher, vocalists Claire Martin and Georgia Mancio, and more. Younger musicians, including Juliet Kelly, Tara Minton, Indira May, Genevieve Racette, and many more, keep the scene vibrant and thriving. These fine musicians can sell out venues, and the illustrious list of names already established as jazz stars proves that making a living as a jazz musician is entirely possible.

# CHAPTER 10

## *The art of communication*

WHETHER YOU ENJOY visual information, reading, or engaging directly with artists or their fan base, there are many ways to engage with jazz, from short videos on social media sites to long and detailed papers and articles in magazines, books, radio station's blogs, and podcasts. There are free online concerts and podcasts; you can go to live performances, read books, listen to jazz on the radio or read columns online. You can pay to attend online concerts if you can't get to one in person—something the pandemic gave us was technological problem solving, which meant those annoying delays when live music transferred to online platforms are largely resolved. Add to this individual musicians' websites, labels' pages, and the endless source of information that is social media, and you can find jazz in whatever format you prefer.

Many people are involved with information sharing, from writers of press releases, books, articles, social media posts, biographies, sleeve notes, liner notes (booklets included with physical purchases), and reviewers.

## CRITIC OR REVIEWER?

THE TERMS "CRITIC" and "reviewer" are often interchanged, but there is a difference. A reviewer writes about the music they hear, concerts they attend, performance, style, artistry, and so on; they write descriptively. A critic will also compare music with historical releases, place it within a historical timeline, contextualize it. Most people, however, refer to both as reviewers.

Reviews are for readers and potential purchasers, not the musicians, but many find value in a reviewer's informed words. The general consensus from musicians is that reviews acknowledge work and show it was good enough for someone to take the time to listen to it and write about it, especially if the reviewer is respected. Even if the review is not favorable, reviewers offer a constructive opinion that can be learned from. They can learn how the music affected those listening, any great things, and anything they found off-putting, like a bum note in the second chorus they missed.

Most musicians say they seek reviews because, as stated above, it shows people notice their music, and if they are positive, they can put them on their websites or direct venue managers to them, so they know the kind of music they play and if they are any good. They will often post the review on social media, directing their followers to them and keeping them in touch with how they are performing. Some musicians are disappointed when a "review" turns out to be their EPK (electronic press kit) rehashed and posted as a "review" with little input from the "reviewer."

The key points made by musicians were:

- Reviews add to the buzz around a new album release. The artists will often have videos, do interviews, announce new collaborations in the press or social media. Reviews add to this general noise made concerning a release.
- They help get bookings. An agent told me that when she is looking to book a band for a tour or residence, she always checks out their reviews to fully understand the audience a band may appeal to (and if they are any good). Reviews are essential for agencies and PR companies taking on new artists because they want to see if their potential clients are likely to succeed.
- Festival curators look to reviews. One told me, "If I did not read reviews, I would only book local artists I could go and see myself and judge if they are going to draw people to the festival. So, of course, I check out reviews. They will be more objective than if I speak to the band or their PR. I can also get information, like who their agent is if they have one, links to their website, videos, etc."
- The reviewer and publication are important. Most musicians try to get interest from respected reviewers who publish on widely read columns or magazines over individuals who post on their sites, simply because the former usually gets a lot more readers.
- Reviews provide artists with quotes they can use on their press pages.

For most musicians, making music is their top priority. Next comes admin for their band and business and all the rest, but reviews are an essential part of the package.

One musician, however, told me he places no value on reviews at all. "There's no such thing as a truly objective review, only a reviewer kidding themselves about their importance."

For those who buy and listen to jazz, reviews can be a barometer to focus their attention. One woman told me, "A genuine reviewer can help listeners decide what to listen to next because it is hard to figure out what's out there given the scary amount of music released each day. The reviewer can be the equivalent of a playlist curator, with the difference that the reviewer can convey with words the feeling of a piece of work, whether an artist is performing well, and so on. They help us navigate to the good stuff."

## THE HIDDEN SIDES OF REVIEWS

NOT ALL REVIEWS are what they seem. Magazines and websites have costs, and they have staff to pay in some cases. They have a website to maintain and other expenses, so unless someone with very deep pockets runs them, it is unlikely they will be publishing reviews without charge (I apologize here to the half dozen I know are run entirely at the owner's cost, but they are in the minority). Most sites take adverts from artists promoting their music, PR companies, or venues promoting their activities.

This potentially creates a conflict of interests. If a label pays for adverts, will a site publish negative reviews of their artists and risk losing their placements? If a PR company advertises its services on a site, will the site publish a negative review of one of its artists? If people pay for reviews and they are all positive, does this dilute their value? If a PR agency is paying a reviewer, will they always give positive reviews of the agency's clients?

Tricky questions. Yet sites need to be able to finance themselves. Most, it has to be said, are fair and allow their reviewers to write the review they feel is appropriate. As a reader, though, it is important to be aware that reviews may not be unbiased. I recently asked a London-based magazine if they would consider a review of an artist, and they replied they would, but only if I could get the artist's label to place an advert on their site.

You might be surprised to learn that most reviewers for online columns do not get paid. They often write for other publications and enjoy the greater freedom allowed in online column reviews than editorial constraints might place on them otherwise. For example, a review for a magazine might have a word count limit of 550 words, while for an online column, the writer might have more freedom of style plus be able to include detail for readers that they cannot include in limited word counts. Of course, not all online columnists are professional writers, but many are. The top online columns enjoy the services of a large pool of contributors who produce high-quality reviews and interviews. For writers, having material online means more people have access to it than if you write for a paper magazine. Reviews in a column can also lead to paid work for writers, so it is a win-win. However, some people accuse online magazines of exploiting naïve contributors by offering them "exposure" for their work, which does not always lead to paid commissions. When I started writing, I came across several ways online magazines obtain articles for free. One offered me "transfer to our physical magazine for paid work" once I wrote three free articles for their online magazine. Of course, they never approved the third free article (which was subsequently published by another magazine). Shortly afterward, another writer contacted me to say this magazine had offered her work once she had written three free articles as a trial. Hmmmm.

Another said they would begin to pay their contributors "soon." Of course, "soon" never came, but I did not realize it never would until I had written half a dozen articles for them. As writers, we do it for the love of jazz, and without volunteer writers, many artists would never get reviewed. It is also lovely if, as an experienced columnist, you help an up-and-coming writer place a review or article on one of the prestigious columns. They get recognition, giving them something to direct editors to if they seek professional work. For the reader, the benefits are good-quality reviews on well-edited and professional-looking sites, but just be aware, they may not be as unbiased as you might hope. It is a case of reader beware.

For musicians, it can be difficult getting a review in the first place. Reviewers can only review so many releases, and online columnists usually have paid work too. As ever, people are willing to exploit the desire to get a review. There are "reviewers" who will offer to review music for a fee. The higher the price, the better the review will be. These services are offered before the "reviewer" even knows what the music is like, which might tell you something about their knowledge of the genre or their dedication to listening and reviewing fairly. Many people are not aware of this practice, but it happens.

Musicians dislike these agencies because they create an unfair marketplace. You can be "brilliant," "5 stars," and "a great new find"—if you can afford it. If a new artist cannot afford to pay for reviews, they may get lost in the vast number of releases each month. The advice is to seek a good reviewer for a well-read column and approach them politely to see if they have time to review your music. Ensure everything is up to date, all the information they need is to hand, and don't send massive mailshots to hundreds of potential reviewers. Instead, use their name and perhaps refer to a piece you read of theirs that you found interesting and say why (see the link to the article at the end of this book). New talent is emerging all the time, and many musicians cannot afford an agent at first, so getting your first review with a reputable reviewer can be crucial. And for the reviewer, it is a beautiful thing to see new artists soar on the back of your review.

# The importance of the reviewer

Anyone can write a review—your mate can put a review on their blog, and it might be a review that is insightful and articulate, but unless your mate is a reviewer known for their integrity, it will not help raise your profile. Certain reviewers, magazine columnists, and bloggers carry more weight than others. Why? It is their knowledge of the music they review and the time they give. There are lazy reviewers who basically rehash an artist's PR notes or EPK and publish this as a "review." This is fine for a listing service but not for a review. Some columns are seen as more valuable than others. These include Something Else Reviews, All About Jazz, Free Jazz Collective, Straight No Chaser, and Platinum Mind. Within the columns, if they have multiple contributors, there are particular reviewers musicians aim for. These include (I am citing names musicians gave me) Brian Morton, John Corbett, Lee Rice Epstein, Peter Margasak, S. Victor Aaron, Hilary Robertson, David Menestres, Martin Schray, Paul Acquaro, Phil Freeman, and more.

It costs musicians and labels money to send copies out for review, too—the physical costs of creating a CD plus postage can add up. If they use a professional writer to create the sleeve notes and liner notes, this also costs. Musicians, therefore, often select reviewers carefully.

Saxophonist and composer Mats Gustafsson told me, "You are the only journalist that I actually worked on getting review copies to. Shall I tell you how many journalists and bloggers beg for review copies every week? I found your texts and approach interesting and thought it important to get you the records. It is expensive for the labels to send review copies, and for me too, and I'm losing royalties if too many copies go for review. I talk to musicians about you, that you are an independent journalist, doing your thing, no matter what, and writing intelligent texts and reviews that mean something. My view on this will not change." From a musician's viewpoint, this kind of sums up why they target particular reviewers. I give this example simply to illustrate a point.

## Do reviews affect sales?

Some people believe reviews are crucial to increasing sales, while others believe they make a negligible difference. A jazz fan told me, "As a music lover, first and foremost, I have bought many albums from reading reviews. Sometimes musicians/bands don't tour or even gig locally, so a review will often lead me to discover music I may not have. If the reviewer shows objectiveness, it is a useful guide for new listeners or music buyers to get the essence of a musician/ album/track. Reviews can be good or bad, but in the end, we all work as one for the common good of jazz, or at least we hope so."

Another musician told me this, "I have a love/hate relationship with critics. I don't put any stock in their opinions, but I realize a good review can keep my band working."

Mind you, another said, "Reviews mean nothing. They got me gigs early in my career, but now I never read them even. It does not matter who writes them; they do nothing to help me get work or support my family. If I pay a journalist for a review, would that make it a positive review? If I paid a magazine for a review or placed an advertisement with them for a review, would it be positive? And if I openly support a journalist, would that mean they would give positive reviews?"

He continued that his relationship was with his fans, not journalists, and he did not want to be in a situation where people might take advantage of him. He is busy with music, family, and friends, and time to read reviews is nil. So some conflicting thoughts here.

One musician told me she got terrible reviews for one album, yet it sold well, and for another, she got terrific reviews, but it hardly sold at all. As a buyer, she told me she relies on reviews. She listens to tracks on streaming platforms before she buys. She dislikes being directed to particular music by algorithms based on the music they think "she might like." She goes to specific sites and reviewers and reads what they think. From these, she finds the music herself and checks it out.

The crucial point is that reviews are permanent. A bad online review can be found years after it was written, so someone looking up your band out of interest might come across a bad review. On the other hand, a good review is also there forever, so putting these on your websites and directing people to go and read them is important. The algorithms of the internet search engines mean that the more people read the good reviews, the higher up the search lists they go, so people googling your band see the good reviews first.

A reviewer agreed with this, saying he noticed that historic posts often randomly get lots of traffic, sometimes connected to a tour or new release by an artist.

Reviews are essential in keeping the release alive—sharing them and using other people's descriptions of your music, not always your own. Many musicians say they see small spikes in sales after a good review and after radio play. A guitarist told me he had met people at gigs who told him they came because they read a review of his recent concerts.

One musician told me that a particular critic always offered scathing reviews of his performances, pouring vitriol and acerbic comments onto the page and awarding his recordings a single star on review sites. This reviewer's reviews stood out from the others, which generally offered excellent reviews and four or five stars. Rather than be upset or ignore the critic in question, the musician began to take the reviews as a badge of honor and quoted extensively from them, especially any inaccurate information. Unabashed, the critic carried on with what became a personal vendetta against this musician until he unexpectedly awarded him a four-star review one day. Even though he liked the higher star value of the review, the musician said he felt a bit annoyed as he couldn't cite the review as his badge of honor.

Even for major stars, reviews are considered more trustworthy than adverts and press releases because reviews are, in theory, objective. Knowledgeable and well-informed reviewers can introduce new listeners to more experimental music, for example, more meaningfully.

Nicky Schrire summed it up when she said, "There's some great writing out there. But in general, I think people either enjoy or steer clear of a journalist based on their personality. It can go either way. I'd rather read a strong opinion piece than a publicized press release."

So, mixed thoughts on reviews from musicians. Yet, I have always felt they must affect sales, and musician David Menestres provided proof.

The chart that follows shows before and after review sales. Journalist Lee Rice Epstein reviewed the music on Free Jazz Collective, and there is a spike in sales after the review's publication in 2020. It helps that Mr. Rice Epstein is a respected reviewer and that the review was published in a much-respected column. Menestres says, "I had a huge spike in Bandcamp streams and sales last summer after Lee reviewed Polyorchard's *Ink* (Out and Gone Music 2020). This is a multi-year graph of streams, but you can see the big increase last summer, largely related to the Free Jazz Collective review."

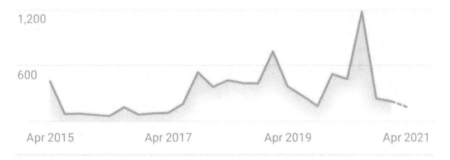

The review was published on July 18th, and there was a spike in sales immediately afterward. The following graph shows the effect of the review even more dramatically, with a spike from just a few to almost 300 plays the day after publication.

From a label's viewpoint, Chris Rand, the head of Lunaria Records explained, "On the whole, I don't think reviews generate many sales. Not in the way you'd expect. The national radio plays often attract people to check out the artist, either on their website or on Spotify. We always see a spike in Spotify streams when a track is played on Jazz FM or Planet Rock, BBC 2/4/6, etc. It does generate great content for social media. Reviews are a way for the artists to get noticed by the editorial and the reader. A good review might lead to a feature or more space given to the artist's follow-up release. And if it's a good review from an expert in that genre, some kudos or affirmation, perhaps. This is all conjecture, but very interesting to see what works. However, today we had a review come in from a Belgian online blues magazine, and a few hours later, I'm posting a CD to Belgium. Every little helps!"

The irony is that even the musicians who say they put no value on reviews ask to be reviewed when they have new music out. I think documentation and having the work acknowledged are important.

A review is a reaction at that time, just an opinion, and you can ignore it if you want to.

## THE COLLABORATIVE NATURE OF WRITING

WRITING ABOUT JAZZ, like everything else in this music, is collaborative. This book starts with me. I am the singular writer of this book. Yet much of what a writer shares relies on so many others. I ask many questions of musicians.

For their replies, the musicians thought about what they were saying, aware that it was for a book to be read globally.

Some of the answers were the musicians' considered opinions, and some included others in a side debate. I read books, academic papers, reports on the music industry, jazz festival reviews, and works cited by the jazz musicians. I remembered conversations, discussions, and quotes and went back to recheck them. The number of people involved in the book directly or indirectly is in the hundreds. Some want to be named, others prefer not to be, and I respect that, especially where they believe their opinions might upset influential people.

A musician draws on many references from those they see playing, teachers, past experiences, and contemporaries. It is never about just one player, though how they play will always be their own interpretation, but the summation of many experiences. A soloist is never truly alone but brings the past and present to their performance. Band members listen and respond to each other. This is collaboration.

Sometimes, when I am researching a musician and delving through accounts, records, and written memories from others in a library or talking to people who knew and worked with them, I can almost feel their presence. For example, talking to the doctor who toured with Sweet Emma Barrett allowed me to understand her character more. She was tenacious and strong. She hated flying, so she booked carriages on a train to get from performance to performance, and she took her food and all her money in a hatbox for the journey. That hatbox stayed with her, even accompanying her on stage because she distrusted everyone. She was robbed of its contents three times. In Quito, Ecuador, I talked with Marvin "Doc" Holladay, who played in Duke Ellington's orchestra. He has strong views about who were the most significant female jazz musicians—all singers—and told me I should include them all in my discussions.

Musicians have told me about times on the road with fellow musicians and little character twists they learned, such as when drummer Terry Day told me about the time pianist Mel Davis walked into a baker's in Holland and started talking to the assistant, assuming she knew who he was. After a while, she said, "Excuse me, sir, if you need some food, go to the back door, and my husband will give you some bread and maybe a cake if you ask. Say I sent you." She thought he was a tramp because he looked so drawn and scruffy. Or the guy who made everyone on the tour bus late because he insisted on diverting to a fish market in Germany.

I have interviewed some of jazz's pioneers, like Peter Brötzmann, one of the first free jazz players in Europe, who is still playing today. Many musicians do not write about themselves but feel able to discuss their opinions and reasons with a journalist. There has to be trust, too, because sometimes musicians reveal personal information, which could be sensational, but a journalist chooses to say nothing because it is not essential for the article and could damage or hurt the interviewee. Revelations, however, provide a deeper insight into their character and what drives them. I can understand their music a little more with the information and hopefully explain some things to readers.

## WHY DO WRITERS WRITE?

TED GIOIA IS a respected writer and author of eleven books. He said, "My main goal is to discover the ways music can serve as a source of enchantment and catalyst for transformative change in people's lives." Ted said this had been his bottom line for many years, and I think this sums up the purpose of writing about music—especially jazz music, which can enchant and transform in an instant.

In my experience, it is about documenting events, sharing the music I am passionate about, and hoping to help others understand the feelings jazz evokes, the good it does, and how it connects us with the past and makes us also look to the future. Plus, I get something out of watching an artist I gave a platform to—whether in a review or on the radio—and seeing them soar—watching what they can do given a chance. For other writers, it is about connecting with people—yes, seeing their name at the foot or head of an article, something permanent. It gives them material to cite when looking for other work. It is also about gaining respect and connection with musicians of immense talent and being part of a community.

# CHAPTER 11

## *Jazz ahead*

IT IS INTERESTING to look back to 1975, when Sidney Finkelstein discussed the future of jazz in the closing chapter of his *Jazz, A People's Music* (Da Capo Press Inc 1975). The author discusses the future of jazz composition and music. He talks of the difficulty of people to be taken seriously when they have been associated with "folk art."

He puts forward possible future situations such as communities sponsoring a large jazz band and encouraging young people to write for them. This had been done with local symphony orchestras. Finkelstein talks of such projects countering the unwholesome atmosphere of jazz—the travel, the late nights, one-night stands, an unsettled home life. He argued that jazz musicians could compose music, and each neighborhood band would have a distinct nature due to the people it attracted, and the community would benefit. The band could play at events such as dances, weddings, etc. Finkelstein states, "fundamental to all of these plans is abolishing all forms of discrimination against minority people, as devastating to our music and cultural life as to our economic life and democracy."

Finkelstein acknowledges such plans are utopian and unrealistic when up against the entrenched canons of music organizations at the time.

In Finkelstein's view, some people would see only local bands, which could be counterproductive because musicians should travel, experiencing different communities and cultures.

People follow fashion, the latest music trend, the big "new thing," and this is natural because each generation wants its own identity. Yet, people also remain loyal to music that inspires them. If everyone only followed commercial, mass-produced music, then folk, opera, and jazz would long since have vanished.

Jazz gives people what they want. It offers noise, excitement, melody, swing, sexiness, and sassiness. It is the reactive music we need. Yet it has changed so much since it was first taken seriously as a genre. It has mixed with cultures worldwide, producing offspring jazz movements that, while still sounding remarkably like their parent, contain elements of different cultures and the voices of many people.

Jazz has been here for a relatively short time yet has woven itself into the fabric of our lives in ways none of us fully realize. Those who play other genres, from Latin, reggae, and hip hop to rap, blues, soul, and rock and roll owe much to jazz because their genre comes from it. Jazz is a precious cultural possession and America's greatest export. However, it is no longer truly American. It has conquered nearly every corner of the world, bringing music that allows emotional content and freedom of expression, and it links local culture to the most influential country on the Earth. Wherever jazz touches, it is richer and becomes warmer.

When one looks around and sees what is happening, there is a resurgence of interest in jazz. Venues on the cusp of closure during the pandemic lockdowns have reopened to packed houses. Many musicians came close to breaking point, and some media faced closure due to the loss of income, but lockdowns made people realize how much they wanted jazz to be there for them and are now taking the opportunity to show their support. All the benefits lockdowns brought us, like outdoor concerts and online events, continue and offer another way to enjoy jazz.

Jazz people proved incredibly resourceful and learned how to expand the reach of jazz without compromising on quality. With online gigs, anyone can now see some of the best musicians in the world performing.

The upsurge of support for jazz has meant the community has grown and become more diverse.

Many musicians play for very little money and have other jobs to supplement their recording or performing live income. Yet, there is an abundance of helpful and knowledgeable people willing to encourage others. They are united by a passion for music and a sense of connection to others. It feels like a community of musicians and music lovers, which welcomes everyone.

Jazz musicians are also encouraged by the reactions of TV, radio, and other media. Jazz is an alternative to the commercial, sanitized music we are often fed. People are not sheep, and they will follow their hearts, and for many, jazz is what moves them. If it isn't, that is also fine.

Jazz has almost surprised people by its resurgence. If we take London as an example, the number of venues that offer jazz solely or as part of their programming is vast. Cafe OTO, Vortex, Iklectic, Pizza Express, The Bull's Head, Jazz Cafe, Ronnie Scott's, Crazy Coqs (Zédel), Piano Bar Soho, 606 Club, and so many other great spaces. In every American city, there are jazz clubs, from NYC's Smalls, Birdland, Blue Note, Dizzy's, Tomi Jazz, Village Vanguard, in New Orleans, Snug Harbor, Preservation Hall, in Chicago Green Mill and the Jazz

Showcase—nearly every city has at least one jazz club. Jazz is incredibly alive, and if you want to see what is really happening, go and see some of the acts or buy a ticket to an online event.

Jazz as a genre has changed. It used to be about muscle and nerve. You might get a gig because of your connections—this is less true today, though it does help to get on the right side of program curators. It used to be you needed to last in a cutting session or outplay the rest in a jam. It used to be you had to be a man. Now it is more sophisticated. It is about what you can bring to the table. It is diverse and stuffed with young people who provide energy not seen since the 1950s and '60s. Musicians including Nubya Garcia, Camilla George, and Laura Jurd prove that being female and young does not hold you back, and jazz today is about ideas, innovation, and pure, unadulterated talent.

Only five years ago, bassist Yaron Stavi told me he had observed that in Europe the scene was younger. Elsewhere, he felt the audience and players were older and not exciting. Between then and now, however, something miraculous has happened. Audiences are as packed with young people as the stage.

I believe initiatives like Keychange and other organizations supporting female musicians show the desire to work toward equality, even if this has not been reached yet. Jazz is working toward this, and funding sources are being made available to jazz musicians that were not accessible before.

French musicians can concentrate on projects because of payments awarded monthly called "intermittence," which helps them with money during the period between paying work, and there is funding to help musicians, which I am not going to go into here because I could not cover every country or fund, and things change readily.

I believe reissues and newly discovered recordings of jazz legends will continue to be popular. These reissues and consistent sales provide money that record labels invest in artists with no guarantee of return. There is also something rather lovely about legends like Coltrane, Monk, Gillespie, Basie, Holiday, and other jazz greats supporting those following.

The future is shining brightly for jazz music. If we look back fifty years, it was rarely taught formally; it was considered American "folk art" and niche. Now it is taught in colleges, played worldwide, and the opportunity to find new music through streaming, marketplace sites, and purchasing physical copies has never been greater. Jazz's ever warm welcome to music from different parts of the world increases its richness, and it is still happening—I recently went to a bass sitar concert, and the jazz was incredible. Different, but incredible.

Musicians love playing to a live audience, but most believe the future will see a mix of live and online concerts. Technology has made it possible for collaborations of musicians to happen in different countries. They can connect and collaborate even when weather conditions or other factors might make travel difficult, and of course, there are no travel costs. There are costs for sound technicians and programs, but musicians believe these performances will remain popular. When people engage in something—for example, clarinetist Adrian Cox began regular "Sunday Services" on a Sunday morning and played music by one jazz great each week and invited guests, providing great entertainment—they will attend regularly.

Young people are bringing jazz up to date with the use of technology, such as apps that allow the listener to mix downloaded tracks, listen to one part such as the sax or bass line, play along and rework tracks on their own devices.

Jazz, like all art, is entertainment. It is made to be enjoyable, listened to, and wondered at. You might forget the music as soon as you stop hearing it, or it might stay with you long after the final note fades, but it is entertainment, just that. It has to be sustainable, and this means artists have to be able to make enough money to remain in jazz. This means being open to change and using opportunities. If we want to keep the diversity of artists, free music is not an option. The music business has to be fair to musicians and fans; otherwise, there will be just a few well-known, protected musicians seen as assets by the labels on streaming platforms. Both musicians and audiences will lose out.

I believe more people realize that while jazz can take on political and social messages and reflect society back at itself, it doesn't have to. You don't have to be different or political to love jazz, and it matters not one iota what you identify as.

Until recently, jazz received little funding, but this is changing as innovators use the music to change the status quo. Terri Lyne Carrington obtained funding for her jazz programs at Berklee and elsewhere, attracting more people to study jazz. Bodies including Help Musicians, the Arts Council, National Endowment for Arts, Pathways to Jazz, Music for All, and many others, offer small or larger grants for jazz projects, and colleges and universities may provide funding as well.

Jazz may be relatively young, but it seems to have gone through many metamorphoses. The young rebels of the 1950s turned into middle-aged, then older, jazz musicians. Now, in the circular manner of things, the vanguard of youth has taken over again, but they are deeply respectful of the elders. The elders support the young, misogyny is becoming passe, and jazz is the music with a spot for everyone.

You only have to take a brief glimpse at the talent that has emerged in the past few years to see how rich and changed jazz music has become. There are some really exciting music collectives—like the Ishmael Ensemble led by Pete Cunningham, Ruth Goller, Kendrick Scott, Ashley Henry, Makaya McCraven, Binker and Moses—new talent is everywhere and creating music that is fierce, free and inspirational.

We are in an age of discovery, and jazz is on the cusp of a new golden era. You should be part of this. So many people are finding jazz and discovering past and present masters for themselves. No one will tell you how to hear or find jazz; it is something you will discover for yourself. Jazz does the work; all you have to do is listen.

Never believe that jazz is not for you or you cannot play jazz. You can if you want to. Don't be sold the lie that jazz is not a career choice. It is. Look around, see the great players of today. That could be you, why not? Over a hundred thousand people attend performances in London Jazz Week. That should tell you jazz is incredibly popular.

Most importantly, don't believe the lie that the music you hear in lifts, as background in films and cafés, is authentic jazz. It isn't—this is just background fuzz. Authentic jazz is played in clubs, it is still developing, and those recordings are captured moments from decades back. Find real jazz and see how different it is. Let jazz inspire your imagination, allow your senses to come alive, inspired by the musicians who play real jazz.

# ACKNOWLEDGMENTS

I AM THANKFUL more than words can say that I can reach out to busy and supremely talented people who are willing to answer my questions: for their openness, willingness to share information, and support what I do. Without the input from musicians, venue managers, educators, agents, radio hosts, and many others, this book would never have been able to investigate on such a level. These people responded to questions, discussed areas, and gave opinions that helped make this book a collaborative and enjoyable journey. So, heartfelt thanks go to the following and many more.

Adam Scrimshire, Aleta Eubanks, Andrea Brachfeld, Andy Quin, Angie Tintanalli, Anthea Redmond, Anthony Cornicello, Anton Hunter, Barbara Douglas Riching, Barry Wahrhaftig, Benny Benack III, Bev Gillespie, Bob Payne, Casper Hoedemaekers, Champian Fulton, China Moses, Chris Beswick, Dan O'Callaghan, David Menestres, Deelee Dube, Duane Eubanks, Elizabeth Surles, Fergus Hall, Freddie Gavita, Gareth Roberts, Gary Fukushima, Gemma Sherry, Gilad Atzmon, Guido Spannocchi, Hannah Horton, Harry James Ballard, Huw Williams, Ian Boddy, Ivan Tenori, Janelle Allbritton, Jason Stein, JB Abbott, Jeremy Price, Joe Higham, John Farley, Jon Opstad, Jon Turney, Jürgen Joherl, Kimberly Cameron, Laura Ainsworth, Laurie Dapice, Lee Rice Epstein, Kate Llewellyn, Lucky Liguori, Luther McGinnis, Mark Miller, Mark Stryker, Martin Johnson, Marvin Muoneke, Matt Parker, Matthew Shipp, Matthias Heyman, Michael Malis, Mike Casey, Mike Neer, Mike Vitti, Monika Herzig, Nathan Holaway, Nigel Price, Nigel Wallis, Nicky Schrire, Pasi Virtanen, Patrick Hadfield, Patrick Naylor, Pauline Black, Pete Cresswell, Peter Slavid, Phat King Cole, Phil Meadows, Philip Booth, Pierre- Emmanuel Seguin, Ray Gelato, Raynald Colom, Rene Aquarius, Rick McLaughlin, Rick Simpson, Robert Swann, Roland Perrin, Rory Clark, Rus Wimbish, Sam Eastmond, Sam Slotsky, Selina Albright, Sheila Anderson, Simon Latarche, Stephen Howard, Stephen Palmer, Steve Lawson, Susanne Alt, Ted Gioia, Thaddeus Tukes, Timothy John, Txomin Dambo, Will Glaser, Yves Leveille. Also the many other musicians, PR managers, agents and labels who gave their time and information. And my editor Richard Sheehan, who has proved both forensic and patient I offer huge thanks.

Special thanks to the following who allowed me to quote from their articles and papers.

Adaso, Henry, "How Jazz Influenced Hip hop," (04/26/19), www.liveabout. com/how-jazz-influenced-hip-hop-2857332

Hall, Fergus, "Making Connections: The Influence of Scottish Traditional Music in Contemporary Scottish Jazz," (2018), www.talkaboutx.net/ xpositionvolume/3/Fergus-Hall

Saraga, Dr. Jonathan, "All Paths Lead To God: A Brief Account Of Spiritual And Religious Faith In The Lives Of Yusef Lateef, Sonny Rollins & John Coltrane," (2019), www.academia.edu/45149065/All_Paths_Lead_To_God_A_Brief_ Account_Of_Spiritual_And_Religious_Faith_In_The_Lives_Of_Yusef_Lateef_ Sonny_Rollins_and_John_Coltrane

Shearn, C. J., "What are the connections between jazz and hip hop?" newyorkjazzworkshop.com/what-are-the-connections-between-jazz-and -hip-hop/

Shipp, Matthew, "Boxing and Jazz," (11/29/10), www.boxinginsider.com/ headlines/boxing-and-jazz/

UK Music, *This Is Music 2021* annual report, (2021), www.ukmusic.org/ wp-content/uploads/2021/10/This-is-Music-111021-v3.pdf

Book typeset by Kate Coe at Book Polishers

Cover art by Ken Dawson at Creative Covers

## OTHER HELPFUL AND INFORMATIVE LINKS

All Party Parliamentary Jazz Appreciation Group, Submission to the Digital, Culture, Media and Sport Committee inquiry into the "The future of UK music festivals" on behalf of the All Party Parliamentary Jazz Appreciation Group, appjag.org/2020/12/13/appjag-submission-to-the-dcms-committee-inquiry-into-the-future-of-uk-music-festivals/

Atzmon, Gilad, "Politics and Jazz," Counterpunch, (20 November 2004), www.counterpunch.org/2004/11/20/politics-and-jazz/

"Boxing and Jazz," Brilliant Corners, A Boston Jazz Blog, (01/2015), brilliantcornersabostonjazzblog.blogspot.com/2015/01/boxing-and-jazz.html

Deflin, Kendall, "Why Jazz Is The Most Stimulating Genre of Music, According To Science," Live for Live Music, (12 June 2016), liveforlivemusic.com/features/why-jazz-is-the-most-stimulating-genre-of-music-according-to-science/

Europe Jazz Network, www.europejazz.net

Farber, Jim, "'It didn't adhere to any of the rules': the fascinating history of free jazz," The Guardian, (7 Sep 2021), www.theguardian.com/film/2021/sep/07/fire-music-history-free-jazz-documentary

F-List Directory of UK Female+ Musicians, thef-listmusic.uk

Girl Plays Jazz Project, girlplaysjazz.org

Interactive Advertising Bureau (IAB), www.iab.com/news/interactive-advertising-bureau-iab/

International Women in Jazz, internationalwomeninjazz.org

Institute for Composer Diversity, www.composerdiversity.com/composer-diversity-database

Kumar, Manisha, "Difference Between Hip-hop and Jazz," Difference Between.net, www.differencebetween.net/miscellaneous/difference-between-hip-hop-and-jazz

PRS for Music Foundation, Women Make Music, prsfoundation. com/funding-support/funding-music-creators/all-career-levels/ women-make-music-2/

Sares, Ted, "Boxing is like Jazz…," International Brotherhood of Prizefighters, (9 May 2016), tss.ib.tv/boxing/featured-boxing-articles-boxing-news-videos-rankings-and-results/22274-boxing-is-like-jazz

stevelawson.net, "Why Bandcamp – Part One," (18 June 2019), www. stevelawson.net/2019/06/why-bandcamp-part-one/

stevelawson.net, "Why Bandcamp – Part Two," (19 June 2019), www. stevelawson.net/2019/06/why-bandcamp-part-two/

UK Music, Music by Numbers 2020 report, www.ukmusic.org/ research-reports/music-by-numbers-2020/

## PHOTOGRAPHER'S WORKS

Jazzcamera.co.uk, www.jazzcamera.co.uk/gallery/main.php

Jazz Photography by Francis Wolff, www.fubiz.net/2015/04/13/ jazz-photography-by-francis-wolff/jazz-photography-by-francis-wolff_0/

Skip Bolen Photography, www.skipbolenstudio.com/archive

The Golden Age of Jazz: The Jazz Photography of William Gottlieb, jazz-photos.com

## INTERESTING READS

Dahl, Linda, *Morning Glory: A Biography of Mary Lou Williams* (Pantheon Books, 1999)

Dahl, Linda, *Stormy Weather: The Music and Lives of a Century of Jazzwomen* (Pantheon Books, 1984)

Ekkehard, Jost, *Free Jazz* (Da Capo, 1974)

Finkelstein, Sidney, *Jazz: A People's Music* (International Publishers Co. Inc, 1989)

Gioia, Ted, *The History of Jazz* (Oxford University Press, 2021)

Larkin, Philip, *All That Jazz – A Record Diary 1961–71* (Faber and Faber, 1970)

Plackskin, Sally, *American Women in Jazz: 1900 to the Present: Their Words, Lives and Music* (Wideview Books, 1982)

Steinberg, Ella, "'Take a solo': an analysis of gender participation and interaction at school jazz festivals", Dissertation (University of the Pacific, 2001)

Stein, Sammy, *Women In Jazz* (8th House Publications, 2017)

Stein, Sammy, *Pause, Play, Repeat* KDP, (March 2021)

## DOCUMENTARIES AND FILMS

*Anita O'Day: The Life of a Jazz Singer*, directed/written by Robbie Cavolina and Ian McCrudden, AOD Productions, Élan Entertainment, 2007

*Charles Mingus: Triumph of the Underdog*, directed/written by Don McGlynn, Jazz Workshop, 1997

*Jazz on a Summer's Day*, Directed by Bert Stern and Aram Avakian, Galaxy Attractions, New Yorker Films, 1959

## ONLINE MAGAZINES AND COLUMNS

Something Else, somethingelsereviews.com
The Free Jazz Collective, www.freejazzblog.org
Jazz Views, www.jazzviews.net
Jazzrytmit, jazzrytmit.fi/wp/
Jazz Possu, rosvot.fi/jazzpossu

## ARTICLES

Gioia, Ted, "Bandcamp Just Got Acquired by a Video Game Behemoth," The Honest Broker, 2 March 2022, https://tedgioia.substack.com/p/bandcamp-just-got-acquired-by-a-video

Stein, Sammy, "Coronavirus, music and beyond," Jazz Views, www.jazzviews.net/coronavirus-music-and-beyond.html

Stein, Sammy, "Primer for musicians: How to engage with jazz journalists," JJA News, 16 January 2022, news.jazzjournalists.org/2022/01/primer-for-musicians-how-to-engage-with-jazz-journalists/

## Recommended recordings

A little bit of everything to get you started.

| ARTIST | ALBUM | LABEL | YEAR OF RELEASE |
|---|---|---|---|
| Charlie Parker | *Bird With Strings: Live at the Apollo, Carnegie Hall and Birdland* | Columbia | 1951 |
| Duke Ellington | *Dance to the Duke* | Capitol | 1954 |
| Charles Mingus | *Pithecanthropus Erectus* | Atlantic | 1956 |
| Miles Davis | *Milestones* | Columbia | 1958 |
| John Coltrane | *Giant Steps* | Atlantic | 1959 |
| Miles Davis | *Kind of Blue* | Columbia | 1959 |
| Charles Mingus | *Charles Mingus Presents Charles Mingus* | Candid | 1960 |
| Ornette Coleman | *Free Jazz: A Collective Improvisation* | Atlantic | 1961 |
| Gil Evans | *Into the Hot* | Impulse! | 1962 |
| Sun Ra | *The Futuristic Sounds of Sun Ra* | Savoy | 1962 |
| Thelonious Monk | *Monk's Dream* | Columbia | 1963 |
| Louis Armstrong | *Hello Dolly* | Kapp | 1964 |
| Albert Ayler | *Ghosts* | Fontana | 1964 |
| John Coltrane | *A Love Supreme* | Impulse! | 1965 |
| Archie Shepp | *The Magic of Ju-Ju* | Impulse! | 1968 |
| Horace Silver | *You Gotta Take a Little Love* | Blue Note | 1969 |
| Albert Ayler | *Music Is The Healing Force Of The Universe* | Impulse! | 1970 |
| Mary Lou Williams | *Mary Lou's Mass* | Mary | 1975 |
| Nina Simone | *Baltimore* | CTI | 1978 |
| Charlie Haden/Carla Bley | *The Ballad of the Fallen* | ECM | 1983 |
| Ella Fitzgerald | *All That Jazz* | Pablo | 1990 |
| Nina Simone | *Compact Jazz* | Mercury | 1989 |

| Earl Hines | *Grand Reunion* | Verve | 1995 |
|---|---|---|---|
| Jason Stein | *Three Kinds of Happiness* | Not Two | 2010 |
| Billie Holiday | *Lady Sings the Blues* | Universal/Not Now | 2013 |
| Soweto Kinch | *Nonagram* | Soweto Kinch | 2016 |
| Jane Bunnett | *Spirits of Havana/ Chamalongo* | Linus | 2016 |
| Jane Ira Bloom | *Early Americans* | Outline | 2016 |
| The Near Jazz Experience | *Afloat* | Sartorial | 2017 |
| Regina Carter | *Ella: Accentuate the Positive* | Okeh/ Sony Music Masterworks | 2017 |
| Esperanza Spalding | *12 Little Spells* | Concorde/ Decca | 2019 |
| Ivo Perelman | *Strings 4* | Leo | 2019 |
| Archie The Goldfish | *Hidden Depths* | Bandcamp/ self-release | 2020 |
| Ed Jones/Emil Karlsen | *Where Light Falls* | FMR | 2020 |
| Shabaka and the Ancestors | *We Are Sent Here by History* | Impulse! | 2020 |
| Matthew Shipp and William Parker | *Re-Union* | Rogueart | 2021 |
| Sons of Kemet | *Black to the Future* | Impulse! | 2021 |
| John Zorn | *New Masada Quartet* | Tzadik | 2021 |
| Hannah Horton | *Inside Out* | Bandcamp/ Apple | 2021 |
| Nigel Price | *Wes Reimagined* | Ubuntu | 2021 |
| Georgia Mancio and Alan Broadbent | *Quiet is the Star* | Roomspin | 2021 |
| Emma-Jean Thackray | *Yellow* | Movementt | 2021 |
| Guido Spannocchi | *Perihelion* | Audioguido | 2021 |

These are just a taste of the diverse range of jazz music available as digital downloads or physical CDs and vinyl.

# Jazz dictionary

Atonal: avoiding the key in which a piece is written. Introduced clashing notes.

Axe: your instrument, even the voice.

Blow: to improvise.

Bop/bebop: fast, solo-led jazz style with rapid chord changes, many key changes, and complexity requiring technical excellence. Often shortened to bop.

Break: a gap in the playing where a soloist takes center stage.

Bridge: the middle section that links two parts of the number, sometimes in a different key or even time.

Chart: a musical score or a part in it (e.g. trombone chart).

Changes: harmonic progression, which results in a chord change.

Chops: the ability to hit the high notes—a slang term for lips, meaning a player, like Louis Armstrong, who could hit high notes. OR it can mean the ability of a player to carry out complex chord changes smoothly.

Counterpoint: combinations of more than one melodic line.

Diatonic: the seven notes of a musical scale.

Dig: to appreciate.

Dissonant: not harmonious.

Head: the first (and sometimes also the last) chorus.

Hip: knowledgeable.

Jam session: an informal group improvisation.

Legit: term for music that is not jazz.

Lineup: personnel of the band.

Mainstream: jazz considered "normal," i.e., not free, fusion.

Meter: time pattern.

Modal: section of a piece in a different key from the next. Modal jazz included sets of different modes.

Modes: the scale.

Noodling: messing about, playing with rhythms.

Outro: an added end section or coda.

Pentatonic: scale where five notes make an octave.

Pocket: perfectly in tune (in the pocket).

Riff: a repeated pattern of notes or rhythm.

Rip: impressive upwards slide on a brass instrument.

Shedding: short for woodshedding—going off somewhere quiet to practice.

Standard: well-known tune.

Timbre: tone quality.

Top: beginning of the chorus.


There you have it—just in case.

# ABOUT THE AUTHOR

SAMMY STEIN IS a reviewer, columnist, and author. She has curated and hosted radio shows, and her books have won praise, including a *Jazz Times* Distaff Award and a place on their Gearhead list. Her *Women In Jazz* book (8th House) won Phacemag's Music Book of The Year award. She is International Editor for the Jazz Journalists Association. She has had work commissioned into the Library of Congress in America, a huge honor for a non-US writer. She writes for Jazz Views, Something Else Reviews, and Free Jazz Collective and is the jazz correspondent for Platinum Mind.

Passionate about jazz music, Sammy curated and organized the London Jazz Platform festival, which showcased acts from the UK, Europe, and America. She has hosted radio series, including *Ladies of Jazz, The Freer Side of Jazz,* and the *Jazz Treasure Trove* for Jazz Bites Radio.

Sammy lives in rural England but journeys far and wide to see and hear music of all genres, with jazz remaining a firm favorite. Her background includes singing—she won folk classes in festivals and played leads in several operas while studying for her degree in botany. She also played the oboe and other instruments before settling on the clarinet and alto saxophone.

Her take on life is that plants and music are some of the greatest gifts we have to enjoy and share. Jazz music unites people, and studying its influence on our society is a never-ending journey.

Citizen Jazz in France called her "the UK expert on diversity in UK jazz." Other comments include:

"Her subjects bridge generations (and international boundaries) to honor the past, assess the present, and point to the future."

Emile Menasche, *Jazz Times*

"It's all here, beautifully written, eloquently argued, clear-eyed in its intentions and open in its invitation."

Jane Cornwell, *Jazzwise* Magazine

"The sheer volume and status of the people who have given up their time to help Sammy, both women, and men, is testament to the respect Sammy has earned across the industry, and the trust people have in her to relay their stories faithfully."

Darren Harper, Jazz Matters

"Ms. Stein writes in a commanding and authoritative style that ensures that the reader's attention is grasped from the outset, and sets out her statements and opinions clearly and concisely before backing them up with solid facts and opinions."

Nick Lea, Jazz Views

"What an incredible book."

Phacemag on *Women In Jazz*